The Hedonism
and Homosexuality
of
John Piper and
Sam Allberry

p.112 makes
? Tennyson a
Marxist

Hartley

1) Unfinished work
of Christ needs
priests

2) God's representative
on earth needs
popes

The Hedonism
and Homosexuality
of
John Piper and
Sam Allberry

—

The Truth of Scripture

Enoch Burke

THE HEDONISM AND HOMOSEXUALITY
OF JOHN PIPER AND SAM ALLBERRY

Published by Burke Publishing, Cloonsunna, Castlebar, Co. Mayo, Ireland.

Scripture quotations taken from the Authorized Version of the Holy Bible.
Any emphases in Scripture quotations have been added by the author.

ISBN: 978-1-9999355-2-8
ISBN: 978-1-9999355-3-5 (electronic)
Cover design by E. Burke
Cover image used with permission

10 9 8 7 6 5 4 3 2 1

For Purchases and Ordering, write to:
Burke Publishing, Cloonsunna, Castlebar, Co. Mayo, F23 W625, Ireland.
For permissions contact: info@thepiedpiperbook.com

Contents

INTRODUCTION

IS THIS THE MOST LAWLESS TIME IN WORLD history? Maybe not. During 18th century England, lawlessness abounded. John Wesley came preaching and living the gospel with such conviction and authority, his followers were dubbed the hedonists. Hedonists? Nay, rather, the *methodists*. The lawless populace of Great Britain saw in this fiery preacher and his followers a zeal for absolute truth and holiness of life that was so pervasive, it resulted in a methodical discipline that reached to every facet of life. Wesley's interpretation of Scripture was not always thorough, but it was meticulous. More importantly, he preached no new gospel but a resurrection of the living relevance of the Scriptures.

Wesley's message was so removed from the apostasy and degeneracy of the age, it drew attention. It was God's answer to man's need. The resulting Great Awakening in England transformed society, and preserved England from the scourge of atheistic socialism that would later afflict its European contemporaries for generations. Historians credit Methodism with a moral regeneration in Britain, as pubs and gambling houses were forsaken for Methodist chapels and observance of the Sabbath day came to characterise a formerly barbarous society. Wesley is said to have travelled 250,000 miles on horseback, preached over 40,000 sermons, wrote or edited 400 publications and left behind a movement with 541 itinerant preachers and 135,000 members. No wonder that as he died, he could declare: 'Best of all, God is with us!'

What can we say of our own time and generation? When is the last time you heard anything close to conviction resonate from the pulpit of a church and knew it was backed by a man who lived methodically what he preached? Where are the preachers whose lives defy the lawlessness of the age?

The Homosexual Issue

The lawlessness of our day has as one of its hallmarks the widespread normalisation of homosexuality. However, the practice of men pursuing other men in lust is not an invention of the 20th century. The first book of Scripture, Genesis, gives a vivid account of two cities characterised by this sin: Sodom and Gomorrah. During His earthly ministry, Jesus Christ referred to the judgment of these cities, destroyed by God with fire from heaven, more than once (Mt. 10:15, Lk. 17:29). The moral law of God, revered first by the Jews and later by the Early Church, explicitly condemned men 'lying' with men as an abomination to God (Lev. 18:22). The writer of the foundational epistle of Christian theology gave specific attention to the passion, act, and penalty of this sin in his preface to the Gospel (Rom. 1:26, 27). Paul mentioned this sin many times in his writings, including referring to those among the believers at Corinth who had practised homosexuality, but were now washed and sanctified (1 Cor. 6:11).

The word homosexual is expressed in the original manuscripts of the Greek New Testament, the *autographa*, by the two words *malakoi* and *arsenokoitai*. These words refer to the passive and active partners, respectively, in homosexual acts. In the Authorised Version, the latter is translated 'effeminate' (1 Cor. 6:9) and the former as 'abusers of themselves with mankind' (1 Cor. 6:9) or 'them that defile themselves with mankind' (1 Tim. 1:10). The two Greek words of 1 Cor. 6:9 can be translated together as referring simply to those who 'practise homosexuality'. The Scriptures, therefore, which describe themselves as *theopneustos*, meaning literally 'God-breathed' or Divinely inspired (2 Tim. 3:16), make explicit reference to the issue of homosexuality. It is not avoided, passed over, or referred to ambiguously. The practice of homosexuality is condemned in the strongest possible terms, in several places in both the Old and New Testaments. This sin, and the lust to engage in this sin, God's Word reveals many times as condemned by Him, dishonouring to the body, and destructive both in this life and in the life to come.

The Anti-Christian Element Within the Church

The theologian J. Gresham Machen declared in 1923:

> The greatest menace to the Christian Church today comes not
> from the enemies outside, but from the enemies within; it comes
> from the presence within the Church of a type of faith and
> practice that is anti-Christian to the core.[1]

Machen's comment was in the context of the modernist controversy of
the 1920s in the United States. He condemned the widespread trend
in churches of accepting as Christians those who rejected the Divine
inspiration of the Bible. This he described as a 'menace' because it
undermined the foundation of truth: Divine revelation.

Today, what is under threat in both church and society alike is not so much
the location of truth (although this is still of ultimate importance) as the
proclamation of truth. In May 2020, for example, the German parliament
passed a law banning the practice and promotion of interventions aimed
at 'changing or suppressing a young person's sexual orientation or self-
perceived gender identity' allowing for fines of up to €30,000 or 1 year in
prison.[2] No religious opposition to the law, sponsored by the homosexual
Health Minister Jens Spahn, was noted in the press. More extensive bans
are being considered in other countries, including the UK and Ireland.

As an aggressive homosexuality seeks to limit the church's freedom,
however, the 'menace' of which Machen warned is alive and well *inside*
the church. Prominent evangelical leaders, far from defending the
faith, are now promoting a transformation in the church's approach to
homosexuality. In the last ten years, the argument that it is possible to be
recognised as a homosexual and a faithful Christian is being popularised
in the church by men such as John Piper and Sam Allberry. This change
of view, which is being particularly promoted by the British Anglican
priest Allberry, is a fulsome attack on the Christian doctrine of sin. The
effect of this new teaching is to undermine Christian teaching on the

sin of homosexuality and so undermine the gospel itself. It is a carefully calculated agenda, as this book will demonstrate, which is having serious consequences in the church across the globe.

Enter the Hedonist

The identity of the two men whose doctrines this book refutes are outlined below.

John Piper is associated with the theological face of evangelical Christianity and has written over 40 books. Piper became well-known on the evangelical scene in 1986 after the publishing of his book *Desiring God: Meditations of a Christian Hedonist*. This popularized a core belief of Piper which he describes as 'Christian hedonism'. Hedonism (for a definition of this term see "The Power of Language" on page 13) has been particularly promoted by John Piper at the Passion Conference. This annual conference is held in Atlanta, Georgia, and features celebrity-style speakers and raucous music under strobe lights. Piper was a keynote speaker at the first conference in 1997 and has been a regular speaker at Passion since then, delivering his message to hundreds of thousands of evangelical youth.

Sam Allberry, who describes himself as a 'same-sex attracted Christian', is currently Editor of the Gospel Coalition and a global speaker for Ravi Zacharias International Ministries. Allberry is an ordained minister in the Church of England and has written several books, including one on homosexuality, *Is God Anti-Gay?*, which seeks to change the Christian view of homosexuality. Evangelical leaders are strongly promoting his book, e.g. in 2014, it featured as one of the 14 free giveaway books for the 8,000 pastoral attendees at the biennial Together for the Gospel conference in Louisville, Kentucky.[3] Since 2013, the book has sold over 100,000 copies.

The popularity of the teachings of Piper and Allberry is not a measure of their truthfulness or spiritual value in the sight of God but perhaps attests to the very opposite. Indeed, the almost hagiographical status which Piper, in particular, has assumed among evangelicals renders his teachings suspect. It was the German Reformer Martin Luther who, in the conclusion of his

Address to the German Nobility, expressed his greatest fear as being that his cause would *not* be 'condemned by men: by which I should know for certain that it does not please God'.[4] The dearth of Christian refutation of the theology of Piper and Allberry serves not as a deterrent but rather an incentive to give their teachings a thorough examination.

This book examines Piper and Allberry from several perspectives:

Chapter 1 sets the stage by investigating the power of language and the importance of words. A rejection is made of Piper's integration of the term *hedonism* with the Christian faith, as well as of the theological sources which undergird Piper's use of this term.

Chapter 2 argues that John Piper's doctrine of Christian hedonism is a revival of mysticism, and thus an implicit rejection of the authority of Scripture, and details the rapprochement of Piper with Roman Catholicism.

Chapter 3 outlines the conflict between the hedonism of Piper and the traditional evangelical understanding of conversion and obedience, with a focus on the redemption of the mind, heart and will.

Chapter 4 examines the teachings of Sam Allberry on homosexuality as presented in his book, *Is God Anti-Gay?* with a specific focus on Allberry's popularisation of the term 'same-sex attracted'. The chapter argues that the new language and attitude towards homosexuality which Allberry advocates are a marked departure from traditional Christian teaching.

Chapter 5 focuses on 3 specific elements of the teachings of Allberry, contrasting them the biblical doctrines of the heinousness of homosexuality, the culpability of the individual and the conversion of the sinner.

Chapter 6 contrasts the irreverence and infidelity of hedonism with the holiness of life which characterised the people of God in times past. The demand in Scripture for chastity of conduct is placed in juxtaposition to the worship and teaching of the annual Passion Conference where Piper teaches.

Finally, **Chapter 7** examines the curse of a careless Christianity and the blessing on those who, like Martin Luther, follow their convictions and take action in the service of God.

Contending for the Faith

Today it is unpopular for any Christian writer to pen anything polemic in nature, i.e. a strong written or verbal attack on some person or doctrine. However, the English word *contend* found in Jude 1:3 ('ye should earnestly contend for the faith'), derives from the Latin word *contendere* which means 'to strive'. To strive for the faith means to demonstrate an outpouring of effort, time and holy zeal in defence of the truth (Jer. 9:3). Not only did Jude exhort God's people to contend for the faith, he urged that they would do so *earnestly*. The Greek word translated 'earnestly contend' is only used once in the Scriptures, here in Jude 3, and is the word *epagonizomai*. It is the word from which our verb *agonise* comes and was used to denote the great effort expended by athletes in contention for a prize. This is the calibre of service in the defence of the faith to which Jude calls every Christian. It is a call to expend every energy and make every sacrifice necessary, despite the pain and hardship, to ensure that the faith we have received is passed on to successive generations.

Yet, how often is this really the case? Professors of Christian belief are today characteristically anaemic, unskilled in spiritual warfare. Discerning minds are rare. Any pretended or real examination of heresy and false doctrine is usually in a 'safe space' where every sentence is predicated with 'bless you, brother'. Faithfulness to Christ and His cause is forfeited in favour of peaceableness. Shrewd judgment of characters, testing of professions, and examination of doctrine and life is almost non-existent. Superficiality in matters of truth is the order of the day. Hands are lifted to worship which refuse to lift the sword against error. Indeed, the only fervour displayed by many churchgoers is in their fulsome and energetic rebuke of the faithful Christians who remain. Machen, a tireless warrior in his day, remarked on the strange anomaly: 'It is strange how in the interests of an utterly false kindness to men, Christians are sometimes willing to relinquish their loyalty to the crucified Lord'.[5] Perhaps it is not so strange in light of the words of our Lord Jesus, who warned that on the last day many would say they had addressed Him as Lord, but whom He would remember only as workers of iniquity or lawlessness (Mt. 7:22-23).

The church today must rise to a defence of the faith, for faith must be defended. It will not defend itself. Proclamation of truth glorifies the living God and is part of the very purpose of creation (Lk. 19:40). Homosexuality is sin. Yes, God did 'rain upon Sodom and upon Gomorrah brimstone and fire from the LORD out of heaven' and yes, it was because of their sexual sin (Gen. 19:24). Yes, homosexuality must be repented of, if one is to enter the kingdom of heaven (1 Cor. 6:9-10). No, homosexuality is not a congenital affliction from which one can never be delivered their whole life long (1 Cor. 6:11). And no, the church does not have to repent of its 'homophobia' any more than the Lord Jesus Christ, who commended the destruction of Sodom (Luke 17:29). Rather, the church must repent of tolerating in its bosom men such as Allberry and Piper whose doctrine is ripping the vitals out of the church's very purpose (1 Tim. 3:15).

Read this book. Then reacquaint yourself with the Scriptures and seek to be effective in the service of God. It is time we rose from our knees, repented of sin, and went forward to do battle with the forces of Satan. Time is short. Eternity is forever.

And the time for excuses is over.

> If thou sayest, Behold, we knew it not; doth not He that pondereth the heart consider it? and He that keepeth thy soul, doth he not know it? and shall not He render to every man according to his works? (Pr. 24:12)

Enoch Burke
Castlebar, Ireland
July 2020

CHAPTER ONE

BEFORE WE BEGIN -

DO WORDS MATTER?

I F PIPER HAD SIMPLY MOUNTED THE PULPIT IN his Baptist church in Minneapolis, Minnesota and urged his listeners to embrace hedonism, it is unlikely that his teaching would have gained the influence it has today. There is something in human nature which recognises that, try as we may, we cannot reconcile hedonism and holiness, pleasure and piety, the world and the church. How then, did Piper achieve the seemingly unachievable?

The Power of Language

The answer is, of course, the way in which all heretics and imposters have ever plied their trade: using the power of language. Piper coined a phrase, and an explanation of that phrase, which succeeded in convincing thousands that his doctrine was true. The phrase is 'Christian hedonism' and the explanation is that 'God is most glorified in us when we are most satisfied in Him'.[1] Not only so, Piper claimed that one must be a Christian hedonist to enter heaven: 'No one is a Christian who does not embrace Jesus gladly as his most valued treasure, and then pursue the fullness of that joy in Christ that honours Him'.[2]

The purpose of a later chapter in this book is to refute the doctrine of Piper from a theological standpoint. Firstly, however, it is important to appreciate that there exists a problem with Piper's doctrine even before one begins to refute his core argument. It is with Piper's use of the word *hedonism*.

The phrase 'Christian hedonism' is like saying 'black white'. It is in itself a hideous distortion of the Christian walk. Christians are those who have rejected hedonism, that is the pursuit of pleasure,[3] to live for Christ their Saviour. Piper's phrase is an invention which cuts the heart out of true Christianity and creates unacceptable confusion.

Nowhere in Scripture is one encouraged to develop a philosophy of Christian living, beyond the instruction which Christ Himself has given: the duty of service (Lk. 17:10; Rom. 12:1). Baptist pastor Nelson Price, who preached the inaugural message before the US President and his cabinet in 1977, once declared: 'Much is said in our society about "celebration" [of Christ]… but there is a much higher form of honour to be given to our Lord. It is imitation…Peter said, "Christ also suffered for us, leaving us an example, that ye should follow His steps" (1 Pet. 2:21)'.[4] Even if Piper insists that by hedonism is meant enjoyment of God, his use of language is still deeply erroneous. By his own words, Piper is a hedonist, and he lives and preaches hedonism.

The purpose of language is to communicate. The power of language consists in its ability to communicate specific meaning and avoid confusion in understanding during spoken interaction. Powerful communicators realise that choosing the right word in a specific situation is critical to accurate communication, with Mark Twain once declaring that 'The difference between the almost right word and the right word is really a large matter – 'tis the difference between the lightning bug and the lightning'. Hence, good writers will often deliberate for hours over the exact words needed to fit the context.

As a teacher of language for many years, I have often reminded students that the meaning of a word can sometimes be more specific than assumed. In English, the word 'student' is often used to describe those in second and third-level study. In German, however, while the word 'Student' is used for students in higher education (e.g. university), it is never used as a term for students in secondary education (U.S. middle and high school). German speakers instead always use the word 'Schüler' in this context. To use the word 'Student' to describe oneself while in secondary school would simply create confusion in the mind of a listener. Conversely, certain words used in German (e.g. the verb 'lernen') carry a more restricted meaning in English. The lesson is simply that the precise meaning of words in their context must be respected if accurate communication is to occur. As we shall see, Piper's use of words shows a disregard for this fundamental rule of communication.

The Words are the Truth

Our attitude towards language reflects our attitude towards truth and reality. A cavalier attitude towards language reflects a loss of conviction regarding truth. So closely does our choice of words reflect our spiritual state and Christian convictions that Christ could declare: 'For by thy words thou shalt be justified, and by thy words thou shalt be condemned' (Mt. 12:37). 'Justified' in this context means acquitted, i.e. pronounced innocent. Christ spoke this statement after warning that what we say arises out of our hearts, and that 'every idle word that men shall speak, they shall give account thereof in the day of judgment'. In this age of ubiquitous cursing and worship of bodily needs, we often hear the phrase: 'You are what you eat'. God says to us, however, 'you are the words you speak'. Your words are you. Even the form in which you speak truth is crucial. If truth is misrepresented, or varnished over with a palatable coating, damnation will result.

To argue for judicious speech in the service of truth is often criticised as vexatious. Some time ago, while visiting a Baptist church near Hamburg in the north of Germany, a congregant told me (I didn't ask!) that the average age of the congregation was 65. I asked her where the sons and daughters of the congregation were. She informed me that some were in the Catholic Church and commented that it was her belief that God did not mind which church people went to, as long as they felt comfortable in it. This was in an evangelical Baptist church, and reflects the state at which evangelicalism is at today. Truth is at an all-time low. So long as a church says they 'love the Lord' (a vacuous phrase), be they Roman Catholic, Universalist or Liberal, and one is comfortable there, so be it!

God's special revelation for humanity is communicated through the words of Holy Scripture. Christians can rejoice that God has given us a perfectly precise communication of 'all things that pertain unto life and godliness' (2 Pet. 1:3). The Lord Jesus Christ while on earth reminded His listeners that every Word of God had precise value and would be fulfilled, down to the last iota: 'one jot or one tittle shall in no wise pass from the law, till all be fulfilled' (Mt. 5:18). Not only so, Christ demonstrated this regard for every word in His discourse with the people when His argument rested on a single word of the Old Testament Scriptures, and the precise meaning attached to that word. In Matthew 22:32, Christ's response to the Sadducees on the resurrection of the dead centred on one word of text: 'I am the God of Abraham...' The precise tense of the word 'am', communicating that God continued to be the God of Abraham, and therefore Abraham still existed, was crucial to refuting the Sadducees' denial of the resurrection.[5] Christians today do well to follow His example, holding every word of God's truth in reverence.

Placing a high value on words, therefore, correlates closely to holding a high view of Scripture. The meticulous Hebrew Old Testament scholars agonised over translation and copying of the Scriptures, lest one word go astray. In the early first century, the Romans tried to persuade Polycarp to deny his faith: 'What harm is there for you to say 'Caesar is Lord'...and thus save your life?' Polycarp's refusal to utter 'mere' words cost him his life.

It was during the Reformation, however, that the importance of words became clearer than ever. The Reformers emphasised four attributes of Scripture, as the revelation of God's truth, which distinguished it from pope and councils. These were the authority, the clarity, the necessity, and the sufficiency of Scripture. The plenary, verbal extent of the inspiration of the Scriptures was affirmed, together with a refutation of all views of partial inspiration.

Piper's Use of Words

In contrast to the Reformers, however, Piper does not afford Scripture a central role in his theology. His book quotes Scripture hundreds of times in an attempt to sound biblical. However, in many cases, Piper is engaging in what is known as *eisegesis*: reading his own meaning into the text of Scripture, rather than interpreting Scripture with Scripture.

One passage quoted more than once by Piper where this is evident is found in Deuteronomy 28:

> Because thou servedst not the LORD thy God with joyfulness, and with gladness of heart, for the abundance of all things; therefore shalt thou serve thine enemies which the LORD shall send against thee, in hunger, and in thirst, and in nakedness, and in want of all things: and He shall put a yoke of iron upon thy neck, until He have destroyed thee. (Deut. 28:47-48)

Piper quotes this passage as proof that 'the Word of God commands us to pursue our joy' because of the reference to service 'with joyfulness, and with gladness of heart'.[6] He prefaces his quoting of this verses by stating that 'the Word of God threatens terrible things if we will not be happy'. This passage, in the view of Piper, is an instruction to the Christian 'be happy' and 'pursue joy'.

An examination of this Scripture in context, however, indicates that this is not a valid interpretation. The verses appear in the middle of a chapter of blessings for obedience and curses for disobedience. Moses is impressing upon the Israelites their duty to joyfully obey the law of God: 'if thou shalt…observe and to do all His commandments' (Deut. 28:1). There is no command to pursue joy or to seek happiness in themselves. Instead, joy and gladness in obedient service to God is the focus. The Puritan commentator Matthew Henry presents the plain meaning of the passage when he makes service and obedience the paramount concern: 'The more God gives us the more cheerfully we should serve him; our abundance should be oil to the wheels of our obedience'.[7] Piper, however, makes no mention of obedience, the intent of Moses, or the context of the passage – the catalogue of blessings and curses made contingent on obedience. Instead, he invests the verses with an alien purpose to support his own doctrine of hedonism.

Piper's misuse of Scripture in this fashion is a feature of his writing. James Rosenquist, in his critical analysis of Piper's doctrine, summarises:

> The weaknesses of Christian Hedonism affect the very core of the system. Piper builds his paradigm on enjoying God as the ultimate ethical concern of the Christian life, a view that is biblically unwarranted. His definition of love is also without biblical support. [...]
>
> Piper has no adequate biblical justification for making enjoying God man's highest ethical obligation.[8]

The lack of biblical warrant for Piper's teaching is of grave importance. Piper's emphasis on hedonism exalts emotion to a place which Scripture does not give it. Instead of beginning with the Scripture and its revelation of truth, Piper orients Scripture around his philosophical view, using Scripture to support his creed of hedonism.

In addition to using Scripture out of context, Piper has, on several occasions, made clear his denial that individual words carry precise meanings. In one of his key works, he writes:

> In this book I will use many words for joy without precise distinctions: happiness, delight, pleasure, contentment, satisfaction, desire, longing, thirsting, passion, etc.[9]

This comment, however, is simply a refusal to acknowledge how language functions. As already noted, one cannot use words without conveying specific meanings. A word conveys a particular meaning whether one intends to convey this meaning or not. No purveyor of words is exempt from the implications of this reality.

Piper, however, seeks to operate outside the rules of language, so to speak, to further his own ends. Speaking at the Ligonier National Conference in 2011, Piper declared:

> And, by the way, just as far as terminology goes, joy, pleasure, happiness, satisfaction, contentment, and the list could go on, I don't distinguish those...definitions are arbitrary, make sure you're clear when you're talking, that's all, clarity is what we want.[10]

Piper here adopts a self-contradicting pose. The only way that any communicator can achieve clarity is to use the right word for the situation, the word that will carry the precise meaning he intends to convey. Piper insists he wants clarity, but in his previous breath has declared that he does not distinguish words. His claim to desire clarity, therefore, is belied by his improper use of words. More serious, however, is what follows, where Piper denies the accuracy and precision of Scripture:

> Just know, that when I read my Bible, I see happiness, I see pleasure, I see satisfaction, I see joy and they're all jumbled up and used interchangeably.[11]

Piper's claim here cannot be taken lightly. To describe the words of Scripture as 'jumbled up' is to deny that the words of Scripture carry precise meaning in their context. To say that Scripture uses words 'interchangeably', in such an indiscriminate fashion, is to lay the charge of imprecision at the feet of Almighty God. This is an outrageous claim. It is to deny God's desire to accurately communicate His will to humanity, as He has done, in the most precise possible way. This assault on the character of God all believers must condemn.

The seriousness of this error of Piper is demonstrated by its clash with the Reformers' doctrine of Scripture in several areas. Hedonism's irreconcilability with the clarity of Scripture and the necessity of Scripture are considered below, while its incompatibility with the sufficiency and authority of Scripture are considered in a later chapter. The Reformers, it must be remembered, held every word of Scripture in high regard. Their insistence that the original manuscripts of Scripture were critical in knowing God's truth led them to reject the Latin Vulgate and call for a return to the original Greek and Hebrew text of the Bible. This *ad fontes* approach, meaning 'back to the sources,' was central to their convictions regarding the precise truth of the Word. The German Reformer Martin Luther testified:

> If the [original] languages had not made me positive as to the true meaning of the Word, I might have still remained a chained monk, engaged in quietly preaching Romish errors in the obscurity of a cloister; the pope, the sophists, and their anti-Christian empire would have remained unshaken.[12]

From this high regard for the very words of the original text, in the providence of God, arose the four cardinal doctrines which undergird the whole system of Protestant theology.

The *clarity*, or perspicuity, of the Scripture means that the knowledge necessary to salvation is presented so simply that those who seek sincerely can find this knowledge by themselves (without recourse to pope, council or priests). The doctrine of hedonism, however, does not arise from a clear reading of the Scripture, nor is it indeed supported by the Scripture at all. The chance of a sincere reader discovering it from the Scripture would be practically null.

The *necessity* of the Scripture was the Reformers' assertion that the Scripture was the divinely appointed means of grace. They rejected Rome's insistence that the Christian had no absolute need of the Scripture. Like Rome, however, the doctrine of Piper devalues the place of Scripture in the life of the Christian. When followed in practice, 'Christian hedonism' reduces the Scripture from being a means of grace to simply being a means to a particular emotional state. For example, Piper describes Scripture in his book as 'kindling for Christian hedonism'.[13] The depiction of Scripture merely as kindling, or scraps of firewood, has the effect of moving one from the words of Scripture to a preoccupation with one's emotional state (hedonism). The reader is subtly steered away from heeding and delighting in Scripture: Scripture becomes merely an aid to reaching an emotional paradise.

Piper's chapter on Scripture in his book contains no emphasis on inerrancy or the verbal, plenary inspiration of the Scripture. Rather, a type of mysticism characterises Piper's approach, as the value of words, language, and accurate thought is denied in pursuit of an emotional goal. Embracing Piper's philosophy generates a dependency, not on the Word, but on one's emotions and the teaching of John Piper. Scripture, with its clarity and necessity undermined, falls to the side.

The Self-Defence of Piper

Several times in *Desiring God*, John Piper defends his use of the phrase 'Christian hedonism'. The first paragraph of his introduction begins by quoting the Westminster Shorter Catechism, drawn up in 1646 to form the basis for the Church of England:

> The old tradition says: The chief end of man is to glorify God *and* enjoy Him forever.[14]

John Piper takes issue with the architects of this document, which has become the most influential church confession ever written. Piper argues, instead, that the theologians should have written, and that his book will aim to persuade, that:

> The chief end of man is to glorify God *by* enjoying Him forever.[15]

Piper neglects, however, to continue quoting from the Shorter Catechism. If he had done so, he would have noted that the Westminster theologians dealt specifically with how God was to be glorified and enjoyed. The second and third questions of the catechism, the questions immediately following Piper's quotation, declare the rule of the Word of God and doing our duty as the *only* sure path to that enjoyment:

> Q2: What rule hath God given to direct us how we may glorify and enjoy him?
>
> A: The Word of God, which is contained in the Scriptures of the

Old and New Testaments, is the only rule to direct us how we may glorify and enjoy Him.

Q3: What do the Scriptures principally teach?

A: The Scriptures principally teach what man is to believe concerning God, and what duty God requires of man.[16]

It is clear from a full reading of the Westminster Confession that the glorifying and enjoying mentioned in questions 1 and 2 were predicated on the belief and duty mentioned in question 3. In the minds of the Westminster theologians, it was impossible to enjoy God without following the 'rule' which He has given to direct us: the Word of God.

The expression of truth

Crucial to the popularity of Piper has been his argument that he is not presenting new truth, so much as a new way of expressing the truth. The Reformers were no strangers, however, to the danger of departing from the language of Scripture even in the mere expression of certain truths. Martin Luther, in response to a disregard by some of the original languages of the Scripture, declared in his letter of 1524 'To the Councilmen of All Cities in Germany That They Establish and Maintain Christian Schools':

> So, I can by no means commend the Waldensian Brethren for their neglect of the languages. … their teaching is so obscure and couched in such peculiar terms, differing from the language of Scripture, that I fear it is not or will not remain pure. For there is great danger in speaking of things of God in a different manner and in different terms than God Himself employs.[17]

The aversion of Luther to using extra-biblical terminology for truth is indisputable. Notwithstanding, this is exactly what the whole doctrine of Piper is built upon. To use the word *hedonism* as a philosophy of the Christian life is most certainly to employ 'different terms than God Himself employs'. None could deny that to do so 'differs from the language of the

Scripture'. Luther, a man mightily used of God in the recovery of truth during a period of spiritual darkness, saw in this approach to teaching a 'great danger'. No doubt his view of this practice was informed by the many times he had stood in debate with the enemies of the gospel, whether at Wittenberg, Augsburg or Worms.

While there are certain words central to the Christian faith which are not contained in Scripture, e.g. the Trinity, these words have been developed by the church in response to challenges in the articulation of already widely accepted truths. Such words, e.g. 'inerrant' in relation to the doctrine of the Divine inspiration of the Scripture, are used for their value in clearly articulating and defending truths from God's Word. This does not mean, however, that every preacher is at liberty to invent new terminology on matters of faith, for a new vocabulary can signify misleading definitions, poor theology, and doctrinal heresy. Paul declared before King Agrippa, not that he had discovered a new philosophy of Christian living, but that he was 'saying none other things than those which the prophets and Moses did say should come: that Christ should suffer, and that He should be the first that should rise from the dead, and should shew light unto the people, and to the Gentiles' (Acts 26:22b-23). This all Christians should be able to say.

The perpetual danger of imprecise speech is that it serves as a smokescreen through which error can enter. The church must ever be vigilant of this threat. This book argues that the doctrine of Piper is incompatible with revealed truth (Jude 4) and a perversion of the faith. It is a doctrine which no pastor could preach, for ministers are exhorted to be 'a pattern of good works: in doctrine, showing uncorruptness, gravity, sincerity, sound speech, than cannot be condemned' (Titus 2:7,8). The commentator William Hendriksen declares: 'His entire speech (his word whenever and wherever it is spoken) … must be sound and incensurable, that is, not open to just rebuke.' [18] How far short of this high standard the teaching of hedonism falls and how great must be the condemnation which follows a disregard of this holy command.

C.S. Lewis and Vernard Eller

In an appendix to the 2011 edition of his book entitled, 'Why Call it Christian Hedonism?' Piper offers a more comprehensive defence of his use of the phrase 'Christian hedonism'. In one of his longest justifications, Piper quotes people 'smarter and older' than him who have 'felt themselves similarly driven to use the term hedonism in reference to the Christian way of life'.[19] Piper then goes on to refer to two men, C.S. Lewis and Vernard Eller, and to quote from their writings.

An examination of these men and what they believed, however, does nothing to support the orthodoxy of Piper's position. Neither of these men could be said to have been blessed of God as examples of Christian service. In fact, both were very much outsiders to the church and their affiliation with the evangelical faith has been strongly critiqued by many. Not only so, the religion of both men was closer to a form of Christian mysticism than the historic Protestant faith.

C.S. Lewis

Piper quotes from C.S. Lewis liberally throughout his book. In the appendix he refers to Lewis' commitment to 'drawing no distinction between the sensual and aesthetic pleasures' in support of his Christian Hedonism, as well as Lewis' comment that 'if this [combining both the aesthetic and sensual] is Hedonism, it is also a somewhat arduous discipline'.[20] Lewis did indeed live and advocate a somewhat hedonistic philosophy of life, this cannot be denied, and it is not surprising to see Piper adopt him as an alibi in his cause.

Many readers of Lewis are aware of his writing and creative abilities, but have little real knowledge of his beliefs. An Anglo-Catholic, Lewis never professed the evangelical faith. He believed in purgatory and attended Roman Catholic confession. Lewis married a divorceé later in life, at a time when divorce was still considered a taboo in Great Britain. Significantly, Lewis' most popular writing, *The Chronicles of Narnia*, was a children's work which served to combine Christianity with magic. This book, which has sold over 100 million copies, includes witches, spells, incantations and enchantment. Lewis' works share elements with those of his close friend, J.R.R Tolkien, author of the mystical *Lord of the Rings*. Tolkien was a devout Roman Catholic, whose works are steeped in Catholicism: he was raised by a Catholic priest (after the death of this mother), his Protestant wife was baptised into the Catholic Church, and his eldest son became a priest.

The craft of Tolkien and Lewis lay in their baneful ability to combine elements of Christianity with mysticism. They can be credited with mainstreaming fantasy literature, particularly within Protestant cultures and among young readers. The scourge of this trend continues today in the astronomical popularity of, for example, J.K. Rowling's *Harry Potter* series, in which she purposely incorporated Wiccan and homosexual elements. Fantasy differs from fiction in that it inspires belief in and derives enjoyment from worlds and creatures that bear no resemblance to those which God created. Thus, it presents to the reader an alternative consciousness as reality. Fantasy also breeds a familiarity with the dark arts, which Scripture condemns (Deut. 18:9-12; Gal. 5:20), including divination, sorcery, witchcraft, and spells. Ultimately, such literature denies the laws of God in the natural world, finding instead spiritual powers in sources which God has forbidden. Fantasy literature's departure from the objectivity of God's natural and spiritual revelation makes it popular with those who pursue meditation, mysticism, and hedonism.

It is no surprise then that Lewis explicitly downplayed the seriousness of sexual misdemeanours in his bestselling book *Mere Christianity*, first published in 1952. Taking a sharp drift away from the Christian theological position laid out explicitly by the apostle Paul in Romans 1, Lewis declared:

> Though I have had to speak at some length about sex, I want
> to make it as clear as I possibly can that the centre of Christian
> morality is not here. If anyone thinks that Christians regard
> unchastity as the supreme vice, he is quite wrong. The sins of the
> flesh are bad, but they are the least bad of all sins. All the worst
> pleasures are purely spiritual.[21]

Lewis here makes an unwarranted distinction between types of sins, i.e. sins of the flesh and spiritual sins. Nowhere is such a distinction found in Scripture. By contrast, Paul links the pride of man in Romans 1:21 with his corresponding slide into practising homosexuality.

Lewis' *Mere Christianity* also betrays an antipathy towards any public deference for the law of God in society. Lewis states, in the context of the responsibility, if any, of Christian members of parliament, that: 'My own view is that the Churches should frankly recognise that the majority of the British people are not Christians and, therefore, cannot be expected to live Christian lives'.[22] To adopt Lewis' approach, as many professing Christians have done, would be to forfeit a strong Christian influence in government and to betray Christian social responsibility. Sadly, since the time of Lewis' writing in 1952, Westminster's legislation has become progressively unchristian and even anti-Christian. In one year, 1967, the Sexual Offences Act legalised homosexual acts and the Abortion Act legalised the murder of the unborn, both a mere 4 years after Lewis' death. It is significant that Piper would use such a man as one of only two witnesses to support his doctrine of hedonism.

Vernard Eller

Piper's second source, Vernard Eller, an American author who died in 2007, was a self-described 'Christian anarchist' and pacifist. Piper quotes Eller liberally in his book,[23] leaning particularly on Eller's discussion of Søren Kierkegaard and his definition of the 'absolute joy' and Eller's comment that the 'sole motive of Christian simplicity is the enjoyment of God himself (and if that be hedonism, let's make the most of it!)'.[24]

What Piper does not tell his readers is that Eller held views well outside the pale of American evangelicalism. Eller, who was Professor of Religion in LaVerne College in California in the 1960s, published an analysis of the Ten Commandments in which he argued that society's moral crisis had come 'not so much because of the old moral standards as because of the moralistic way those standards have been presented'.[25] Eller advocated a rejection of what he termed *moralism*: the 'handing down of edicts in an arbitrary, authoritarian, no-nonsense sort of way' and argued for a new way of presenting Christian morality. His writings contain a wide familiarity with unchaste terminology for all types of sexual immorality; one of his later books is entitled *The Sex Manual for Puritans*. Eller's unseemly use of sexual language is obvious from the title and amounts to a blatant rejection of the spirit of the Old and New Testaments.

Like C.S. Lewis, Eller frowned upon Christians significantly influencing politics. His book *Christian Anarchy* denied there was any such thing as 'a Christian-biblical morality' and decried the involvement of Christian leaders in politics. Eller declared that it was 'improper to designate any particular, detailed, and exclusive political strategy as being the one Christian means of getting us to a goal' using as an example that 'no, it is not the place of the church to specify, regarding abortion, what is the only law of the land that will be acceptable as moral and right'.[26] This view has not been accepted by Christendom, in general, as being anywhere close to the teaching of Scripture.

Piper, perhaps influenced by Eller and Lewis' antipathy towards significant Christian involvement in politics, has counselled against pastors encouraging congregants to vote on particular political initiatives.[27] He refused to advise his own congregants how to vote when an important amendment protecting marriage was put to public vote in his state of Minnesota in 2012. Piper stated in a sermon before the vote 'Don't press the organisation of the church or her pastors into political activism' and the vote was later lost by the slenderest of margins (a swing of 1.9% of voters).[28]

Both Lewis and Eller, rather than having been privy to some great secret of Christian living, instead forfeited Christian duty and a public defence of God's law in their embrace of hedonism. Their writings served more to adapt Christianity to the age than to conquer the citadels of the age for God. The mysticism and pacifism of their hedonistic beliefs, as will later be demonstrated, were a clear departure from the traditional

Protestant faith in the authority of the Scriptures. Notably, as churches and individuals have adopted this hedonism, they have renounced their salt and light responsibilities to the world around them and become instead a reflection, morally and spiritually, of the world itself, squeezed willingly into its mould.

Words Matter

Words do matter. To depart from the language of the Scripture is to depart from the historic doctrine of the Reformers and the authority of the Scriptures. One's use of words reveals one's respect, or lack thereof, for the only infallible source of truth: every word of God (Mt. 4:4). Piper's introduction of a new term into the church, and a mystical and sensual one at that, signifies a rejection of the clarity and sufficiency of Scripture. No longer does the Christian have enough in the Bible to teach him how God would have him live: instead he needs a copy of *Desiring God*. In the company of men such as C.S. Lewis, Scripture becomes merely a means to an end, with the end being a mystical pursuit of emotion which bears no resemblance to the Christianity of the Bible (Gal. 1:6-7).

The prophet Isaiah, speaking during a time of consternation and upheaval in the land of Israel, faced the same fantasy-peddlers that we do today:

> And when they shall say unto you, Seek unto them that have familiar spirits, and unto wizards that peep, and that mutter: should not a people seek unto their God? (Isa. 8:19a)

Isaiah rejected the mysticism proffered to him because he had something far better: the sure words of the living God. To him, indulgence in witchcraft and wizardry was an absurdity to be shunned, as well as a portent of deep darkness:

> To the law and to the testimony: if they speak not according to this word, it is because there is no light in them. (Isa. 8:20).

Words are important. That one's words accord with God's words is the only real indication of light in the soul. If one's words do not accord with God's words, Scripture itself testifies that only perpetual darkness awaits the soul (Isa. 8:22b).

The rest of this book will look at how, behind the words chosen by Piper, lies a dark doctrine which negates the authority of the Scriptures and is ushering in the demise of the church.

CHAPTER TWO

JOHN PIPER:

PREACHING

MYSTICISM,

NOT CHRIST

J OHN P IPER DEFINES HIS DOCTRINE OF HEDONISM AT the close of the introduction to *Desiring God* as a 'philosophy of life'.[1] By his own admission, Piper has made this philosophy the cornerstone of his life. He describes himself in transformative terms as having been 'converted to Christian Hedonism'[2] and 'become a Christian Hedonist'.[3] He acknowledges that his philosophy has 'touched virtually every area' of his life.[4] Not only so, Piper condemns those who do not subscribe to his philosophy saying that 'it is unbiblical and arrogant to try to worship God for any other reason than the pleasure to be had in Him'.[5]

Piper's philosophy has all the hallmarks of a religion: conversion, a new identity, pervasive belief, and a strong sense of exclusivity. Piper's religion of hedonism, however, does not fit within biblical Protestantism. It is not Protestant for one overarching reason: it establishes emotion, and not Scripture, as the ultimate authority for its adherents.

The question of where or to whom to go for truth looms large in all major religions. The word which is used by Protestants to describe this is authority. Put simply, if something has authority, then to ignore or disobey it is to disobey God. One's authority is what one listens to, and where one finds the truth by which one lives.

For Christians, of course, the Scripture is the authority. To disobey Scripture is to disobey God. The Christian 'listens to' Scripture, as it were, holding this Book as his only source of infallible truth.

Mysticism: Emotion is the Authority

Mysticism, however, exalts emotion to a place of authority. The measure of one's rightness with God becomes something within the person, something subjective. Satisfaction, pleasure, and desire replace the 'obedience of faith' (Rom. 16:26). John Piper declared no less at Passion 2020 when he stated:

> If the name and fame of Jesus does not become your greatest desire, you will not only waste your life you will lose your life.[6]

Losing one's spiritual life is here made contingent on a hierarchy of desire. This is classical mysticism. The foundation of Piper's theory of hedonism is rooted firmly in knowing one's 'desires': Piper claims that everyone must be a hedonist, that everyone must seek pleasure, and that there is 'no need to choose between duty and delight in the Christian life'.[7]

When you use the word 'desire', it can have several meanings. Should you say that you 'desire' chocolate, it could mean that you love eating chocolate, or that you want (or choose) chocolate. Naturally, the first is an emotion, the realm of the heart, and the second is a choice, the realm of the will. When John Piper uses desire, he is using it in terms of the former. He means an emotion, a state of happiness and pleasure. He seeks to transform his emotional state, so that he is a happier being. Piper's doctrine of hedonism is predicated on the authority of emotion. Emotion, in the final analysis, is supreme. One's emotional state is what will determine one's spiritual destiny.

To exalt emotion to a place of spiritual authority is not a novel idea. Various figures through church history have pursued this route, particularly prominent figures within medieval Catholicism. Church historian Earle E. Cairns mentions Bernard of Clairvaux, Catherine of Siena and Meister Eckhart as either philosophical or psychological mystics who pursued an 'experience of ecstasy…[or] an emotional unction with Deity by intuition'.[8] In modern secularism, mysticism has revived in popularity. Buddhist practices rooted in mysticism, with its emphasis on inner spirituality, have been actively promoted by secular governments as a replacement for Christianity. Mindfulness, meditation, and yoga are now aggressively marketed to schoolchildren as avenues to spiritual health. Such practices share with Piper's hedonism a mystical emphasis on desire. The American Buddhist monk Bhikku notes:

> All phenomena, the Buddha once said, are rooted in desire. Everything we think, say, or do—every experience—comes from desire. Even we come from desire. We were reborn into this life because of our desire to be. Consciously or not, our desires keep redefining our sense of who we are.[9]

The centrality of desire observed in Buddhist spirituality is, as previously mentioned, also a core tenet of Piper's philosophy. Like Buddhists, Piper views desire as an end, rather than a means to an end. In a section of his book entitled 'Worship as an End in Itself', Piper declares no less than seven times that feelings are an end in themselves.[10] This is the emphasis of mysticism: feelings become the goal of life.

The emphasis in Scripture, however, is repeatedly on the will and obedience as an end, and not on the emotions. God's desire is for His people to be obedient, holy, and righteous as He is. This is communicated throughout Scripture (1 Pet. 1:15; John 14:23; Titus 2:12; Gen. 18:19; Heb. 11:5; James 1:25, 2:22, 24; 3:13). This is not to detract from the fact that feelings are important. But to establish emotions as all there is, or even as the primary element in the Christian experience, is unfaithful to the Scripture, Christian doctrine, and church history.

Over 30 years ago, Christian philosophy professor Arthur L. Johnson warned of the threat which mysticism posed to the very foundation of Christian belief, the Scripture, in his book *Faith Misguided: Exposing the Dangers of Mysticism*. Writing only two years after the publication of Piper's *Desiring God*, Johnson did not mention Piper or his doctrine in his book. He did, however, lament what he saw as a trend among professing Christians to make emotions a 'test of truth' or even 'the reality itself':

> When we make feelings the means of gaining knowledge, or
> when we make them a test of truth, or when we come to see them
> as the reality itself, then our emotions become misdirected. The
> repudiation of mysticism is not the denial of proper emotions.
> Instead, it is the assertion that reason, not emotion, is the tool for
> grasping and testing truth.[11]

Johnson saw in mysticism a departure from God's means of revelation
in the Scripture. His concern was that mysticism was 'an open door to
false doctrine' because it established an alternative source of authority, an
alternative basis for truth.[12] For Johnson, the danger to the church was
compounded by the fact that mysticism, this 'misdirection of emotions' was
'rapidly gaining favour in secular society'.[13]

Piper, of course, claims to hold Scripture as the only authority, but in
reality, his emphasis on emotion makes Scripture fade into the background.
In general, false teachers do not overtly deny the authority of Scripture or
replace it completely with another authority source. Rather, the authority
of Scripture is 'squeezed out' by giving so much authority to another source
that it effectively overshadows the Scripture. The American theologian
Loraine Boettner understood this when he declared:

> We need only read church history to discover that when another
> source of authority is placed alongside Scripture as of equal
> importance, Scripture eventually becomes relegated to the
> background. Whether that other source be reason, emotion, or
> tradition, the inevitable result is that it supplants Scripture and
> causes it gradually to fade away. If that other source be reason, we
> get rationalism. If it be emotion, we get mysticism. And if it be
> tradition, we get ecclesiastical dictation or clericalism. In each case
> the Bible, while still given lip service, is effectually superseded.[14]

The mysticism incorporated in Piper's hedonism is a clear example of
emotion superseding the Scripture. Of course, as Boettner well notes, the

Bible is still given lip service. However, the end result of the philosophy of Piper is to deny the Scripture any authoritative voice in the everyday life of the believer. A follower of Piper's teaching, as with one of the medieval mystics, will inevitably be consumed with their own feelings, not with the objective instruction of the Scriptures. A hedonist 'listens' to his desires. Emotion is his authority, and mysticism is the result.

If Piper has a low view of the authority of the Scripture, and shares with Romanism a proclivity for another source of authority instead, one expects that he would be sympathetic towards the Roman Catholic position. This is indeed the case. Piper's commentary on and attitude towards all things Roman Catholic suggests not only a strong sympathy for Rome's position, but almost a longing for their fellowship. Indeed, there is little to suggest that Piper is, at heart, separated from Rome in anything but name as his doctrine of hedonism sits far more snugly within the Roman framework than within his proclaimed evangelicalism. In fact, Piper's doctrine is likely serving as a conduit to bring those who were once fiercely opposed to Rome's heresies back into its fold.

The Reformers: Scripture is the Authority

The authority of Scripture is acknowledged by church historians as being the formal, or core, issue of the Reformation. The word formal means that this quarrel was at the heart of the matter, despite not being always directly in the limelight. This was in contrast to the material issue of the Reformation, the issue which stood at the forefront, that of justification by faith. The Reformers' rallying cry therefore became Sola Scriptura and their spirit that of Isaiah 8:20 – 'To the law and to the testimony'.

The Reformers' insistence on the final authority of the Scripture lies at the core of the spiritual and social implications of the Reformation. The message of the Reformers was manifestly practical, springing as it did from the objective truth of Scripture rather than subjective tradition or emotion. Philip Schaff, the noted church historian, chronicles this in his magisterial work on the German Reformation:

> Faith, in the biblical and evangelical sense, is a vital force which
> engages all the powers of man and apprehends and appropriates
> the very life of Christ and all his benefits. It is the child of grace
> and the mother of good works. It is the pioneer of all great
> thoughts and deeds.[15]

Words such as 'force', 'engages', 'powers', 'appropriates', 'works', and 'deeds'
leave Schaff's reader in no doubt as to the vitality of Sola Scriptura. It
was the ultimate example of a good tree bearing healthy fruit (Mt. 7:17).
Not only did this great doctrine rejuvenate personal morality and rescue it
from the broken jars of mysticism and clericalism, it rejuvenated society.
Schaff, commenting on the Reformers' doctrine of the priesthood of the
laity, noted its major contribution to the development of civil liberty:

> [This doctrine] makes every member of the congregation useful,
> according to his peculiar gift, for the general good. This principle
> is the source of religious and civil liberty which flourishes most
> in Protestant countries. Religious liberty is the mother of civil
> liberty. The universal priesthood of Christians leads legitimately
> to the universal kingship of free, self-governing citizens, whether
> under a monarchy or under a republic.[16]

As has been observed in an earlier chapter, the social contribution of
mysticism is exactly the opposite: Piper's heroes Lewis and Eller embody
a withdrawal from the public sphere, and a refusal to resolutely pursue the
general good in the public square.

The Reformers' embrace of the Scripture as the ultimate authority meant a
steadfast rejection of all other competing sources, whether mystical experience
or church tradition. Luther, for example, did not just cast off the shackles of
Romanism: he also rejected completely the alluring overtones of mysticism.
He was no stranger to them, for before his defence at the Diet of Worms in
1521, he encountered mysticism through his counsellor Johann von Staupitz.
Having examined its offerings, he found it unsatisfactory. Schaff notes:

But mysticism alone could not satisfy him, especially after the Reformation began in earnest. It was too passive and sentimental and shrunk from conflict. It was a theology of feeling rather than of action.[17]

For Luther, 'feeling rather than action' was a heresy to flee. It had no practical offering to the problems of his age. Luther would not settle for a feeling in the stomach in his battle with pope and councils. Only the Scripture could be his stay.

It was the Reformers' unshakeable adherence to their doctrine of the Scripture that ushered in a sure foundation for personal and social change. It was a revival of the Scripture to its rightful place and a sweeping away of all that corrupted the pure Word of God. Schaff records that Luther 'repudiated the mystic doctrine of the inner word and spirit [and] insisted on submission to the written letter of the Scriptures'.[18] The result was a revival of preaching, of studying the Word, and of true religion. It was a restoration of the New Testament model, which assumed that Christians would be students of the Word, apt to learn even those things from Scripture which were 'hard to be understood' (2 Pet. 3:16).

Theologians detect in the revival of mysticism an abandonment of the authority of Scripture. Johnson argues that mysticism is a retrograde spiritual step, a departure from certainty in matters of truth and a 'rejection of the heart of Protestantism'.[19] To seek truth in mysticism is to reject the God of Israel, who in the days of the prophet Isaiah appealed to Israel's reasonable faculties: 'Come now, and let us reason together' (Isa. 1:18). The Christian does not deny the role of emotions in human experience, but he or she does insist that Scripture is the only infallible guide if one is to 'grow in grace and in the knowledge of our Lord and Saviour Jesus Christ' (2 Pet. 3:18). As Johnson summarised: 'The Word, which must be understood, is the ultimate criterion of truth. Subjective experience is not an adequate basis by which to judge the truth of anything'.[20]

Piper's Affinity with Rome

If Piper's beliefs on authority clash with the doctrine of the Reformers, as I argue, one would expect that Piper would have much less conflict with Roman Catholicism than the Reformers did. This is indeed the case. In fact, Piper's mystic hedonism is leading evangelicals on a fast trot back to Rome, where mystics have long nestled under its skirts.

There is little common ground between hedonism and the Reformers' doctrine of the sufficiency of the Scripture. The former is a philosophy of the Christian life which does not arise from a study of the Scripture. The latter, by contrast, is the teaching that the Scripture contains all that is needed to come to know God and to obey God perfectly. No other source of knowledge beyond Scripture, including psychology, can give the believer any greater insight into how to live aright with God. The Reformer John Calvin wholly repudiated any departure from this strong position:

> Those who, rejecting Scripture, imagine that they have some peculiar way of penetrating to God, are to be deemed not so much under the influence of error as madness.[21]

Calvin explicitly condemned the formulation of 'new doctrines' by ministers:

> We conclude, therefore, that it does not now belong to faithful ministers to coin some new doctrine, but simply to adhere to the doctrine to which all, without exception, are made subject.[22]

The incompatibility of hedonism with the doctrine of the sufficiency of the Scriptures is corroborated by Piper's amicable relationship with Romanism, which invests extra-biblical tradition with equal and greater authority than that of Scripture. This is clear from two main areas: Piper's statements on the pope, the head of the Roman Catholic Church, and his corresponding refusal to recognise authority as the main issue dividing Roman Catholicism from biblical Protestantism. What follows is an examination of Piper's incriminating statements on both issues.

On the Pope

The pope, also known as the 'bishop of Rome' or the 'Roman pontiff', is the final arbiter on all matters of truth for Roman Catholics. The residence of the pope is in the Vatican City, an enclave within Rome which was established in the Lateran Treaty (1929) between the Holy See and Italy, under fascist dictator Benito Mussolini. The pope has not only teaching authority over the Church, but governmental authority. The First Vatican Council (1869-1870), where the primacy of the pope was established, declared the teaching authority to extend to 'the church dispersed throughout the whole world' and the governmental authority to be 'the divine assistance promised to him [the Pope] in blessed Peter, that infallibility… in defining doctrine concerning faith or morals'.[23]

The Protestant repudiation of the papacy has long been one of its most definitive features. The gulf between biblical Protestantism and Roman Catholicism on this issue has only intensified since the Reformation. In 1870, at the First Vatican Council, Pope Pius IX formally defined the 'infallibility' of the pope as an issue 'upon which the strength and coherence of the whole church depends' and declared anybody 'who said it was not so… [to be] anathema'.[24] At the Second Vatican Council, which began in 1962, Pope John XXIII called all Christians to return to the 'Holy Mother Church under the Roman Pontiff.'

In the late 1800s, the historian Schaff vividly described the practical dimension of the papacy: 'an aged Italian priest shut up in the Vatican controls the consciences of two hundred millions of human beings…and rules them with the claims of infallibility in all matters of faith and duty'.[25] While the nationality of the pope and the number of Roman Catholics has since changed, the essential reality has not: the bishop of Rome defines the beliefs of the Catholic Church. Whether they like it or not, all Roman Catholics must submit to the authority of the pope in all things spiritual. The centrality of this doctrine in Roman dogma holds a demonstrable influence over individuals and nations who pledge allegiance to Rome, a practical influence which Protestants often fail to recognise.

The Reformers and the Papacy

The Reformers were under no illusion as to their fundamental quarrel with the papacy, and they opposed it on two fronts: because of its practical odiousness and because of its suspect theological foundation. Luther opposed the pope by degrees; his opposition became more and more overt as his conviction of the sole authority of the Scriptures increased.

It was the issuing of 'Exurge, Domini', described as 'the papal counter-manifesto to Luther's Theses [which] condemned in him the whole cause of the Protestant Reformation',[26] which ushered in the final break. Luther fervently opposed the bull, labelling Pope Leo X as a 'hardened heretic, an antichristian suppresser of the Scriptures, a blasphemer and despiser of the holy Church'[27] and, while throwing the bull into the fire on December 10, 1520, declared, 'As thou [the Pope] hast vexed the Holy One of the Lord, may the eternal fire vex thee!' Schaff characterises the bull as propagating an 'intellectual slavery' and, indeed, Luther's rejection of such slavery only deepened with the passing of time. 'The devilish papacy', Luther said, 'is the last evil on earth, and the worst which all the devils with all their power could contrive'.[28] The papacy had come to epitomise all that Protestantism was against: intellectual bondage, theological error and blatant hypocrisy.

John Calvin's later theological rejection of the pope in his *Institutes of the Christian Religion* focused almost entirely on the issue of authority. Calvin examined the Roman Catholic use of Matthew 16:18 ('Thou art Peter, and upon this rock I will build my church') and refuted the pope's claim to special authority. Calvin argued that the 'whole of Scripture is repugnant' to the assertion that the church is built on Peter.[29] He noted that the promise of Christ to feed the church through Peter (John 21:15) was also given to his colleagues (2 Cor. 5:18) and was given by Peter to others (1 Pet. 5:2). Calvin also observed that Peter was treated by his colleagues as 'their equal and colleague, not their master', that the Apostle Paul in his epistles never mentioned a supreme pontiff in his description of the church and its leadership, and that there was no scriptural record of Peter officiating as a bishop at Rome.[30] Rather, Calvin portrayed the pope as having 'impudently transferred to himself the most peculiar properties of God and Christ',[31] referencing Scripture's repeated clear statement that there is only one Head of the church, the Lord Jesus Christ (Eph. 1:22; 4:15; 5:23; Col. 1:18; 2:10).

Piper and the Papacy

The energy which characterised the Reformers' opposition to the pope is conspicuously absent in Piper's pronouncements on the same. When asked in 2009 what he would say if he had two minutes with the pope, Piper did not mention the authority of Scripture but said, 'I would say, "Could you just, in one minute, explain your view of justification?" And then on the basis of his one minute, I would give my view of justification'.[32] Piper did not say that he would charge the pope with aggregating to himself authority that belongs only to God. Notably, Piper's answer did not deal with the issue of authority at all, the formal issue of the Reformation. Instead, Piper answered that he would discuss justification with the pope, and not authority, because 'papal authority…seem[s] to be maybe a little more marginal than going right to the heart of the issue'.

This answer, from a theologian of years standing, is deeply concerning in that it shows that Piper has little quarrel with Rome on the fundamental issue of authority. What energised the Reformers in their struggle against the papacy was their celebration of a re-established source of authority which belied the claims of the pope. Calvin boldly declared that 'properly speaking Christ did not give this power to men, but to His word, of which He made men the ministers'[33] and defied his detractors to find any testament to a pope in Scripture: 'let the Romanists, therefore, seek their primacy somewhere else than in the word of God, which gives not the least foundation for it'.[34]

The issue of authority, namely the Scripture versus tradition and the papacy, was the chasm between Protestantism and Romanism, a chasm to which all other disagreements were subject. By contrast, Piper's proclivity to initiate a discussion with the pope on justification indicates a low view of any disagreement on authority. For a true believer, a discussion could not even begin with the pope, as such would be pointless. The pope is operating out of a different mindset. One could only point out the presumptuous sin of that mindset, unless, of course, one was tacitly in agreement with the pope on authority. Could it be that Piper's grievance with the pope is not on authority because Piper himself has departed from the sufficiency of the Scripture? This sin Piper could not raise with the pope because it is a sin on which he has built his own doctrine of hedonism.

Not only so, on several occasions, Piper has tweeted statements regarding the Vatican indicating that he holds a firmly optimistic view of this bastion of popery. In 2013, Piper tweeted a prayer that God would 'put in place a Pope most willing to reform the Catholic Church in accord with your most holy word'. This tweet tacitly accepted the legitimacy of a pope, and the authority that is bound up in the very definition of the pope as the 'head' of the Catholic Church. Such a prayer would be impossible for John Calvin who declared the papacy to be 'a perverted government, compounded of lies, a government which partly extinguishes, party suppresses, the pure light...a chain to bind us in idolatry, impiety, ignorance of God and other kinds of evil'.[35]

This is not Piper's only tweet on the Roman hierarchy. In 2014, Piper referred to the Pope's rebuke of careerism amongst the hierarchy as embodying the spirit of his own book on ministry: 'Brothers, We are Not Professionals'. In 2018, as scandals engulfed the Vatican, Piper tweeted his suggested 'qualifications for the new Pope'.

The amicable tone of Piper's tweets is far removed from the abhorrence of the pope and his cardinals which Calvin had in his day:

> For a long period, the Roman pontiffs have either been altogether devoid of religion, or been its greatest enemies... [they] with almost the whole College of Cardinals, and the whole body of their clergy, are so devoted to wickedness, obscenity, uncleanness, iniquity, and crime of every description, that they resemble monsters more than men.[36]

Is Authority All-Important?

Piper's commentary on Roman Catholicism at Desiring God particularly undermines the area where the Protestant position is strongest: the authority of the Scriptures. In a 2016 article advising somebody facing 'temptation to move toward the Roman Catholic Church', Piper treats the issue of authority as if it is one of weakness for Protestants, when indeed the exact opposite is the case. He says: 'Don't at that moment just take the issue of authority into account and leave all the other doctrines aside'.[37] Piper counsels not to 'isolate' the issue of authority, instead advocating a wider approach. Piper, however, is moving Protestants away from their point of strength and the most monstrous fault of Rome. The reality is that true Protestants will always isolate the issue of authority. This was the Reformers' cry, Sola Scriptura, the formal cause of the Reformation.

Men of God throughout the history of the church have faithfully emphasised that authority is the all-important issue. The late John Gerstner, Professor of Church History at Pittsburgh Theological Seminary and author of *A Primer on Roman Catholicism*, declared 'Rome has substituted for the doctrine of the perspicuity [clarity] of the Scriptures the doctrine of the audacity of the Church'.[38] For Gerstner, Rome had made the error of errors, the error of thinking it could not err.[39] In opposition to Rome's heresy, Gerstner exegeted 1 Timothy 3:15 to prove that it is the Scripture which gives the church authority, not the other way around:

> Incidentally, the expression that the church is the pillar and ground of the truth does not point to a pillar on which truth rests, but to a pillar on which truth was posted for public announcement in antiquity. In other words, it refers to the church as witness to the truth and not the basis of it.[40]

Piper, however, would dialogue with Rome's Pope without tackling this greatest of Rome's errors. This approach, for a true believer, would be akin to the proverbial 'rearranging deck chairs on the Titanic'. It would amount to a discussion on truth, with no agreement as to where one finds truth, or what source one listens to, i.e. no agreement on authority. Such a dialogue would end in chaos, unless one agreed with Rome that a final authority for truth can reside in an extra-biblical source. The cardinal rule to which all believers must return is the Scripture: 'To the law and to the testimony: if they speak not according to this word, it is because there is no light in them' (Isa. 8:20).

In a further article published in 2018 on his website, Piper argues in a conciliatory tone that devout Roman Catholics can be Christians. He downplays the guilt of the Roman hierarchy at the outset: 'I do not mean that Roman Catholicism has a corner on that kind of misleading teaching' – unusual, considering the size of the Catholic Church and the magnitude of its errors.[41] Throughout this article, Piper uses the word 'concerned' when speaking of Rome, which does not fit with the biblical pronouncement of anathema (damnation) on those who preach a false gospel (Gal. 1:9).

Piper's core argument is that devout Roman Catholics can be saved if their 'true heart embrace of Jesus is better than their mental ideas or doctrines'. But for the Christian truth is received by way of 'mental ideas or doctrines'. The heart embraces what the mind receives: there is no other avenue to repentance (Rom. 6:17). Scripture speaks about salvation as being a response to preaching; thus, one's grasp of Christ is inseparable from one's doctrine. Notably, Piper is not arguing that Roman Catholics can be saved if their personal doctrine clashes with that of Catholic dogma. Instead, he is propagating clearly unbiblical teaching regarding those in subservience to a false gospel. Of course, Piper's hedonism is fully compatible with Roman Catholicism, for both make something other than Scripture an authority on truth, in order to continue in sin.

Conclusion

The hedonism of Piper is a false philosophy which diverges from Christian doctrine at a critical vertex and assaults the very foundation of the Christian faith: the authority of the Scripture. It must be utterly rejected by all who profess the faith 'once *delivered* to the saints' (Jude 3, emphasis added). Luther's concluding statement regarding John Eck at the Leipzig Disputation in 1519, where the core issue at stake was where authority ultimately resided, could also be said of Piper:

> I am sorry that the learned doctor only dips into the Scripture as the water spider into the water – nay, he seems to flee from it as the Devil from the Cross. I prefer, with all deference to the Fathers, the authority of the Scripture, which I herewith recommend to the arbiters of our cause.[42]

A man who merely dips into the Scripture is a man to avoid. The Christian embraces it. God's commandments are his delight (Ps. 119:143). Living and proclaiming the authority of God's Word is his holy duty. It has been said of the Church of Rome that she 'advances in proportion as Protestantism degenerates and neglects its duty'.[43] Today, the prosperity of men such as Piper is testament to the fact that the church of God does not know and proclaim the truth as it ought, or even as it once did. 'No longer', as Gerstner said (who himself was raised in only a nominally Protestant home), 'does the Protestant church ring with the great themes of salvation by grace, the authority and genuine inspiration of the Bible, a divine Christ, and a final judgment. We must humbly confess that to a great degree we have been false to our true gospel and that Rome has been true to her false gospel'.[44]

This is a confession that is long overdue. It is a confession, however, that must be escorted by action. It is time to reject the water-spider teaching of Piper's hedonism and take up, once again, the cry of Luther: Sola Scriptura.

CHAPTER THREE

PREACHING CHRIST,

NOT MYSTICISM

JESUS CHRIST IS THE CENTERPIECE OF SCRIPTURE. The risen Christ conversed with two unwitting disciples on the road to Emmaus and 'beginning at Moses and all the prophets, He expounded unto them in all the scriptures the things concerning Himself' (Luke 24:27). A true emphasis on the only source of authority, the Scripture, will always result in an exaltation of Christ and an appropriation of His saving power (Jn. 1:12). Conversely, where no authority exists, powerlessness in the Christian life will result.

Several years ago, I spent a morning removing some old cabinets from the walls of a kitchen. Having disconnected the electricity, or so I thought, I began the hard work of removing the cabinets. However, in the process of trying to pull free the extractor fan, with my head in a confined space between the top of the cabinets and the ceiling above, there was a flash of light and a deafening bang. The fan had been on a different electric circuit than the one disconnected, and had, unknown to me, still been live with 220V electricity. After an initial shock, I had an overwhelming sense of relief. God had mercifully kept me unharmed, despite an unwitting tug-of-war with a lethal source of power.

It is one thing to experience power where one least expected it; it is arguably more common today, however, to witness no power where power ought to be. Such powerlessness over sin, which is sadly widespread amongst today's professing church, is a result of fraudulent preaching and a departure from the Scripture. Church history demonstrates that when any authority other than the Scripture usurps the reins of the church, the result is a glorification of a man, or a method, rather than Christ, and a concurrent loss of spiritual power and purity of life. Heretics have always one thing in common: they aggrandise their own profile to 'draw away disciples after them[selves]' (Acts 20:30) rather than to bless the church through preaching Christ as Lord (2 Cor. 4:5). As already considered, Piper's hedonism does not exalt the power of the living Christ, but the broken cistern of mysticism. Its powerlessness to impart change has the same track record of success as its sister, Roman Catholicism.

Nowhere was the powerlessness of false spirituality clearer than at the time of the Reformation. The heretical doctrines of Rome had almost fully obscured the glory of Christ and the power of His salvation. Corrupt popes and bishops grew fat on the church, while spiritual darkness was the plight of the masses. Today, the exterior facade of Rome may be whitewashed anew, but the same anti-Christ doctrines adorn its Catechism. For the millions of adherents who serve it faithfully, it closes the door to Christ and hinders those who would enter in (Luke 11:52). It was Gerstner who said of Rome, when detailing the consequent errors of her denial of God's Word:

> Most important of all, Rome closes the divine way of salvation.
> She has taken Christ from us and we know not where she has laid
> Him... we are in bondage again; we are yet in our sins.[1]

To be 'yet in one's sins' brings a curse and not a blessing to an individual, a church or even a country. The apathy, decadence and indifference to spiritual matters that pervades predominantly Catholic countries today, such as the Republic of Ireland, continues to speak to the true nature of Romanism.

Like Romanism,[2] Piper's hedonism is 'another gospel' than the gospel of Christ (Gal. 1:9). Its exaltation of emotion and desire draws the sinner away from Christ and into self. Ultimately, Piper forsakes the simplicity of service to Christ and preaches 'another Jesus' whom Paul and the Reformers did not preach (2 Cor. 11:2). In place of objective deliverance from sin, comes subjective dependence on emotions; in place of freedom comes bondage, a bondage to pleasure. Piper's denial of the sufficiency of Scripture is a denial of the sufficiency of the Christ of Scripture, the Christ whom Paul preached: 'Christ in you, the hope of glory: Whom we preach, warning every man and teaching every man in all wisdom; that we may present every man perfect in Christ Jesus' (Col. 1:27-28).

A living proclamation of the authority of Scripture over against all competing authorities exalts the crucified Christ. Faced with the religiosity of the Jews, on the one hand, and the philosophy of the Greeks, on the other, Paul declared:

> But we preach Christ crucified, unto the Jews a stumblingblock, and unto the Greeks foolishness; but unto them which are called, both Jews and Greeks, Christ the power of God, and the wisdom of God. (1 Cor. 1:23-24)

When one departs from faithful exposition of the Scriptures, the preaching of Christ departs with it. When one trades the Scriptures for philosophy and mysticism, the simplicity of the cross becomes foolishness, an affront to human intelligence. Christ may remain as a figurehead, a role-model, or an inspirational figure, even a Saviour; but He has been stripped of His central role. He no longer has the pre-eminence He is due as the ruler and possessor of men (Col. 1:18). Boettner rightly delineates the place of Christ in Romanism:

> The Roman Church teaches the deity of Christ. But it places Mary and the priest as mediators between Him and the believer, so that there is no way of access to Him except through them. He is usually presented either as a helpless babe in His mother's arms or as a dead Christ upon a cross. In either case He is effectively removed as a strong, virile, living personality, or as a daily companion or Saviour who hears and answers prayer. He has little to do with the problems of everyday life.[3]

So also, with the philosophy of hedonism, there is a subtle yet clearly perceptible shifting of the soul from a simple obedience to Christ. Instead of focusing on the glory of Christ, hedonism focuses on the power of pleasure. Truth is to be enjoyed rather than obeyed. Adherents of Piper's philosophy become like what they worship: hypnotised by the machinations of Piper, they live as those under a spell. Their testimony is not the shout of victory in Christ. Instead of being consumed with love for the Saviour and a determination to follow in His footsteps (Phil. 3:8-12), the hedonist turns their gaze inwards and becomes consumed with themselves. Knowledge and dedication are supplanted by emotionalism and sentimentality. The voices of hedonists do not ring with clarity on the Fall, sin, conversion, Christ and coming judgment. What was said to the erring Galatians could be said to them:

> O foolish Galatians, who hath bewitched you, that ye should not
> obey the truth, before whose eyes Jesus Christ hath been evidently
> set forth, crucified among you? (Gal. 3:1)

Two areas in which the preaching of Christ crucified must be firmly re-established are those of conversion and obedience. Piper's mysticism has clouded these great doctrines with new language, new ideas and new emphases. In the process, mysticism has triumphed, truth has been obscured and God's people have been robbed. A clear refutation of Piper's doctrines in light of Scripture, and a restatement of what Scripture teaches in both of these areas is necessary.

Hedonism, Christ and Conversion

> *And Zacchaeus stood, and said unto the Lord: Behold, Lord, the half*
> *of my goods I give to the poor; and if I have taken any thing from any*
> *man by false accusation, I restore him fourfold. And Jesus said unto*
> *him, This day is salvation come to this house, forasmuch as he also is a*
> *son of Abraham. For the Son of man is come to seek and to save that*
> *which was lost. (Lk. 19:8-10)*

In mysticism, the focus is on unity with the Divine; in Scripture, it is on conformity to God's righteousness. Hedonism changes men to pleasure seekers, grace to bondservants of Jesus Christ. One is manifested in feelings, one in choices. Perhaps no two systems of belief could be more diverse. It is no surprise, therefore, that a clear example of Piper's divergence from Christian doctrine is his philosophy of conversion.

One of the best treatments of how the gospel transforms the will is found in the work of the late Linleigh J. Roberts. In his book *Let Us Make Man*, Roberts conducts a biblical study on the nature of man, his sin problem, and his remaking in the gospel. His aim is to demonstrate how salvation transforms man in his entirety, so that he chooses to do God's will.

In chapter 12 of his book, Roberts deals with the application of redemption to the will. He explains salvation as having an effect not just on the mind and the heart, but also on the will, so that man chooses to obey God. Roberts rightly observes that a change in the will cannot be conjured up from inside, but only from outside the person. In his book, he contrasts what he describes as the Objective View of the will with the Mystical View. The latter popular view sees the will as completely free, whereas the Objective View is biblical. Roberts explains:

> What are the objective factors in the operation of the will ignored by the mystical view? The will does not operate autonomously and independently of the mind and the desires. A man simply cannot choose against, or in opposition to, what he knows and desires. [...] As the apostle Paul says, an unregenerate man lives in the lust of the flesh, doing the desires of the flesh and of the mind (Eph. 2:3). Our Lord taught that a corrupt tree brings forth corrupt fruit; no matter what it does, it cannot, in and of itself, produce good fruit. In other words, it is impossible to get a righteous decision from an unrighteous character.[4]

In other words, the human person cannot change what he or she longs for, this must first come about by a change in the mind and heart. Roberts continues to clarify how this change comes about:

How is it possible then, for a sinner to make a right decision for Christ when that decision is opposed to his own unrighteous character? It is a decision which is completely contrary to his knowledge and his desires. Just as it took a supernatural agent to get Adam to decide against God, it takes another supernatural agent to get sinful man to decide for God. If there is to be a genuine conversion, the Spirit of God must renew the will and thereby enable a person to embrace Jesus Christ.[5]

While Piper, dealing with conversion in his book, mentions the need for man to be enabled to obey God, this is not his focus.[6] Rather, he climaxes his chapter on conversion with an interpretation of Mt. 13:44. Piper argues that 'something happens in our hearts before the act of faith…a new taste has been created – a taste for the glory of God and the beauty of Christ'.[7] This is a departure from Christian doctrine, for Piper does not say that this is a conviction of the mind that engages the will with a desire to please and obey God. Rather, the 'taste for the glory of God and the beauty of Christ' is left hanging as a mystical concept in the air, intangible, effervescent, and biblically unrecognisable.

Piper's emphasis is not the emphasis of Scripture. His focus is not the focus of the godly in ages past, such as King David who said 'I will praise thee with uprightness of heart, when I shall have learned thy righteous judgements' (Ps. 119:7). For David, joy was as much or more a product of obedience, as the other way around. Piper preaches a different message, even by his own acknowledgement, for he says:

How does this arrival of joy relate to saving faith? The usual answer is the fruit of faith. [...] But there is a different way of looking at the relationship of joy and faith. [...] Before the decision comes the delight. Before trust comes the discovery of Treasure.[8]

This may sound appealing to some, but even Piper cannot seem to find biblical precedent for changing the historic Christian interpretation of mind, emotion and will. Piper appeals to Hebrews 11:6 to bolster his theory of conversion, i.e. that regeneration is connected to a new desire for pleasure in God:

> But without faith it is impossible to please Him: for He that cometh to God must believe that He is, and that He is a rewarder of them that diligently seek Him. (Heb. 11:6)

Piper presumptuously assumes, however, that the 'reward' in this verse is a pleasure or some analogous emotional sensation on the part of the believer. This is without foundation. A true believer knows that great reward to be confirmation of acceptance with God, the approval of God on their lives and the surety of His blessing. This is established by the preceding verses, where both characters, Abel and Enoch, received clear confirmation that they were accepted of God: Abel 'obtained witness that he was righteous' (Heb. 11:4) and of Enoch it was said that he 'was not found, because God had translated him' (11:5).

Roberts and other Christian theologians held to the historic Christian interpretation of salvation as a transformation of mind, heart and will. Indeed, the language used to describe this change often includes words such as illumination and inclination. Illumination is the work of the Holy Spirit in convincing the sinner of sin. Inclination refers to God giving the sinner an interest in the things of God and a desire to please God. Roberts, unlike Piper, did not merely say that the desires of man needed a new focus, or a new object of desire, rather they needed a thorough-going renewal:

> When he has information and illumination, he has the right knowledge for a sound or wise decision. He might not be inclined to act upon it, however. His desires must be renewed also. When we give him a demonstration of the love of God, the Holy Spirit

brings the *inclination*. As Solomon prayed, 'that He may *incline* our hearts unto Him, to walk in all His ways, and to keep His commandments, and His statutes, and His judgements, which He commanded our fathers' (1 Kings 8:58, emphasised). When information, illumination, demonstration, and inclination come together, the result is *motivation*.[9]

This complete renewal of the heart is the work of the Holy Spirit. God brings the inclination, not man. Furthermore, it is not, as Solomon knew, an end-in-itself but a springboard to obedience. When the mind is convinced and the heart is inclined, the will is then engaged to walk in God's ways and do His service.

Hedonism, Christ and Obedience

> *And Jesus said unto him, No man, having put his hand to the plough, and looking back, is fit for the kingdom of God. (Lk. 9:62)*

One of the seven reasons which John Piper gives for writing his book is his belief that 'affections are essential to the Christian life, not optional'.[10] Piper contrasts affections with decisions, saying that decisions 'require so little transformation to achieve' and are 'evidence of no true work of grace in the heart'. Ultimately, Piper's argument is that the affections are a better test of Christianity than decisions of the will. The import of his words is to move Christians away from an examination of their obedience to God's commands to a nebulous fixation on their emotional state.

Scripture, however, regularly exhorts obedient decision-making and depicts the same as a significant indicator of grace. The examples are manifold:

> Joshua 24:15 – 'Choose you this day whom ye will serve; whether the gods which your fathers served that were on the other side of the flood, or the gods of the Amorites, in whose land ye dwell: but as for me and my house, we will serve the LORD.'

Esther 4:15, 16 – 'Then Esther bade them return Mordecai this answer, Go, gather together all the Jews that are present in Shushan, and fast ye for me, and neither eat nor drink three days, night or day: I also and my maidens will fast likewise; and so will I go in unto the king, which is not according to the law: and if I perish, I perish.'

John 6:68, 69 – 'Then Simon Peter answered Him, Lord, to whom shall we go? Thou hast the words of eternal life. And we believe and are sure that Thou art that Christ, the Son of the living God.'

Decisions can be made without grace, as indeed the discipleship of Judas clearly shows, but this does not negate the value in God's eyes of a decision made to follow Christ (Luke 15:10). Indeed, the whole book of Daniel illustrates the power of God that accompanies purposeful decision making (Dan. 1:8; 3:16-18; 6:10). Likewise, in the New Testament gospel of Luke, the glory of Zacchaeus' conversion climaxes in the decisions that he took (Luke 19:8).

John Piper leans on the 18th century theologian Jonathan Edwards to bolster his case for the primacy of emotions. Piper quotes Edwards' comment on 1 Peter 1:8 ('believing, ye rejoice with joy unspeakable and full of glory') that 'true religion, in great part, consists in the affections'.[11] However, Piper does not exegete the verses preceding 1 Peter 1:8. Yes, the recipients of Peter's letter had 'joy unspeakable' but Peter knew this because of the 'trial of your faith…tried with fire' (1:7) which they were successfully and faithfully enduring. Far from having a trite joy, these same recipients were in 'heaviness [or grieved] through manifold temptations' (1:6). Their joy was not a fickle pursuit but a by-product of praiseworthy dedication to Christ, even to the point of death.

Jonathan Edwards was right when he declared that the 'new birth really brought into being a new nature that had new affections' (this is basic Christian doctrine). However, Piper adds to Edwards' words:

> We are commanded to feel, not just to think or decide. We
> are commanded to experience dozens of emotions, not just to
> perform acts of willpower.[12]

The error of Piper's argument here lies in the breath of importance which
he attaches to emotions. Scripture does command us to certain feelings
(Rom. 12:12, 15; Eph. 4:32; 1 Pet. 1:13, 2:2), but the vast majority of its
commands make no reference to feelings whatsoever. Piper references less
than 30 verses in his list of texts, but the New Testament contains over
1000 individual commands or exhortations. There can be no doubt that
the intent of such commands is that man's will conform to God's law. This
is emphasised by the expositor A.W. Pink, who notes that the word *law*
occurs in Romans no less than 75 times:

> Obedience to the law of God is man's first duty... that is why
> in the first of the Epistles [Romans], the Holy Spirit has
> taught us at length the relation of the law to sinners and saints,
> in connection with salvation and the subsequent walk of the
> saved...that is why sinners (Rom. 3:19) and saints (Jas. 2:12)
> shall be judged by this law.[13]

Piper attempts to see 'underneath' each command in Scripture a command
to feel but it simply isn't there. God demands obedience. Even when Piper
says, 'Though joyless love is not our aim, nevertheless it is better to do a
joyless duty than not to do it, provided there is a spirit of repentance for
the deadness of our hearts' he reveals that his aim is always joy and not
duty. [14] This is an aim which has no grounding in Scripture, but rather is a
philosophical invention. Piper's weak view of obedience has consequently
led to his followers neglecting or even rejecting duty, and instead judging
their parents, grandparents, brothers, sisters, and other church members for
their 'lack of emotion' in Christian service.

Emotions change, but decisions can hold the soul fast. One cannot exactly
decipher how Daniel's emotions were as he stood at the edge of the lion's

den before he was shoved in, lions snarling below, or what strength of feeling the three Hebrews possessed as the heat of the furnace slew the well-armed guards. What matters was their decision to obey God. Their courage to follow through set for God's people a timeless example of Christian service.

The Strength of Obedience

The individuals in the hall of faith are not there because of the tenacity of their 'desire for God'. They are there because their faith showed itself in obedience. They are there because they believed that God existed and that diligently seeking Him brought incomparable blessing. They are there because their wills and God's will were perfectly aligned. Not only were their minds convinced and their hearts inspired, their wills were engaged in mighty activity for God. Their faith was seen in obedience.

The Scripture does not dwell on one's motives, but rather on one's beliefs seen in action. It does not emphasise strength of desire but strength of character. On the wall of the classroom where I teach, I have affixed a poster in prominent view of both my students and I. The poster reads:

> Watch your thoughts, for they become words.
>
> Watch your words, for they become actions.
>
> Watch your actions, for they become habits.
>
> Watch your habits, for they become character.
>
> Watch your character, for it becomes your destiny.

The Christian view of character, of course, is different to that of the world. Firstly, it begins and ends with a personal faith in Christ (Rom. 1:17; Heb. 12:2). Secondly, it is characterised by steadfast obedience despite challenges (Rom. 5:3). Suffering for Christ is readily embraced, amid the testing and tribulation of an evil world, and patient endurance in this builds character (Rom. 5:4). The poem is a daily reminder that it is the holy 'monotony' of small obediences, as it were, that counts with God. This, rather than the shortcuts of mysticism, is the key to a joyous hope and a fervent love (Rom. 5:5,11). Here alone lies the pathway to lasting strength of character.

Scripture presents multiple examples of true faith. Abraham 'offered up Isaac', not because of a hedonistic pursuit, but rather because of his unshakeable faith in God. Abraham obeyed because he 'account[ed] that God was able to raise [Isaac] up' i.e. he was convinced of the Almighty God's power to resurrect from the dead (Heb. 11:17). Joseph believed the promised Exodus was coming ('[He] made mention of the departing of Israel' – Heb. 11:22), as did Moses ('He had respect unto the recompense of the reward' – Heb. 11:26). Rahab was assured of the spies' upcoming victory (she 'received the spies with peace' – Heb. 11:31). Their unshakeable assurance of God gave them unshakeable strength for God. In Christianity, the heroes are not the mystics but the doers of the Word (vv. 32-40).

John Piper's philosophy of hedonism ('God is most glorified in us when we are most satisfied in Him') begets weakness rather than strength. Nowhere in Scripture does God instruct us to seek pleasure. Rather, we are instructed to seek God and His wisdom and strength (1 Chron. 16:11; Pr. 2:1-5) Nowhere in Scripture are we instructed to assess the extent to which we are 'happy' or 'satisfied'. Nowhere in Scripture are we informed that God is most glorified in us by a particular form of obedience. Where no such particulars have been revealed, our aim ought to be to 'do all the words of this law' (Deut. 29:29). Indeed, Scripture is replete with instruction to us to assess, not our 'satisfaction', but how much our lives conform to God's law. Doing so brings an increasing strength, as the Christian grows in God's grace.

There is a simplicity to the Christian life as presented in Scripture. In the Parable of the Sower, the singularity of the true believer lies in their hearing and understanding the Word and bearing fruit, 'some an hundredfold, some sixty, some thirty' (Mt. 13:23). The emphasis here is not on the initial or emotive response to the preaching of the Word. Indeed, the true Christian is contrasted with an earlier unregenerate hearer who 'with joy' receives the Word but bears no lasting fruit (Mt. 13:20). Rather, the emphasis in Scripture again and again is fruit. In the long run, the wicked prove unfruitful (Mt. 13:22). The one defining characteristic of the Christian is fruit.

There are various synonyms for fruitfulness used in Scripture. One of these is strength. The godly Old Testament King Hezekiah lamented that at a time of national crisis, Israel was not in the place of blessing with God which she ought to have been. The metaphor he employs captures the tragic fruitlessness of Israel's state: 'children are come to the birth, and there is not strength to bring forth' (2 Kings 19:3). Rabshakeh, the blasphemous king of Assyria who was reproaching the God of the Hebrews, should have been no match for a nation whose God was the Lord. However Israel, because of disobedience, was weak, and forfeiting the blessing and fruitfulness it might have enjoyed. The tragic metaphor is one of spiritual weakness incurred through disobedience to God.

The lack of strength in today's church has the same cause, and the solution is not some psychological trick but a return to the commandments of the Lord. King David rejoiced on many occasions at the strength he enjoyed when in the right place with God: 'For Thou hast girded me with strength to battle: them that rose up against me hast Thou subdued under me' (2 Sam. 22:40). For David, God was the 'God of my strength' (Ps. 43:2; cf. Ps. 46:2; Ps. 144:1). Several of David's psalms rejoice in the strength he enjoyed when faithful to God (Ps. 8:2, 68:35). The elect are characterised, overwhelmingly, not merely as people of erudition or scholarship, but those 'whose strength is in Thee…They go from strength to strength' (Ps. 84:7; cf. Pr. 10:29).

It is little surprise that strength is the one quality most lacking in the church today, for it has been torn out of the Scripture by 'pastors' keen to replace it with mysticism and feelgood tricks. Meanwhile, the church is impoverished, robbed of truth and robbed of the blessing of truth obeyed. An obedient people are strong. Truly wise people are empowered through God to defy the gates of hell: 'A wise man scaleth the city of the mighty, and casteth down the strength of the confidence thereof' (Pr. 21:22; cf. Pr. 24:5).

The Lord did not tell Gideon to go in his 'hedonism' to save Israel from her foes: rather He declared, 'Go in this thy might, and thou shalt save Israel from the hand of the Midianites' (Judges 6:14; cf. Joshua 14:11). Where are those who have so long meditated upon the commandments of God that they are strong to face the foes of the 21st century? Too many are apologising for God's truth almost before it is out of their mouths, displaying weakness, not strength, in the moment of battle. How far this falls from the character description we find in God's Word: the house of the wise man when embattled 'fell not: for it was founded upon a rock' (Mt. 7:25).

The Weakness of Hedonism

By contrast, spiritual weakness in Scripture is always synonymous with disobedience. The account of the first declension in the book of Judges is a pattern which appears again and again throughout the history of the people of God:

> And the children of Israel did evil in the sight of the LORD, and served Baalim: [...] And the anger of the LORD was hot against Israel, and He delivered them into the hands of spoilers that spoiled them, and He sold them into the hands of their enemies round about, so that they could not any longer stand before their enemies. (Judg. 2:11, 14).

Rejecting the God of their fathers, who had revealed Himself to them time and again, the Israelites turned to false gods, disobeyed God's law, and faced the judgment of God: defeat at the hands of their enemies. God, the source of their vigour, withdrew Himself from them and gave them up to their enemies, who were inevitably stronger than they were.

Having moved the church from Scripture with its sure and steadfast 'anchor of the soul' (Heb. 6:19), one of the primary effects of hedonism has been to popularise a blasé approach to lust in the church. Piper's followers become hedonists. Bewitched (Gal. 3:1) into an embrace of a 'spiritual' hedonism, and a treacherous 'pursuit of pleasure', they take their first steps on a perilous path. For many, there is no safe return. Lust always ruins its victims. Samson in Scripture is the great example of how even a believer is no match for the power of this sin. Andrew Fausset, the 19th century Bible commentator, warns no less: 'Fleshly lusts war against the soul. Yet men flatter themselves they can toy with the temptress, and not be entrapped'.[15]

Piper's doctrine does not openly advocate a hurried embrace of lust. However, it does introduce its beguiled adherents to the pathway thereto, for it exalts desire, pleasure and happiness to pedestals where God never intended them to be. Piper's followers are induced into a shared commonality with the world, which also seeks pleasure (1 John 2:15) and so separate themselves from the love of God. Familiarity with sin leads to ensnarement, judgment and spiritual death (1 Cor. 3:17). Fausset summarises this truth in his exposition on Samson's life and demise, portraying the gradual nature of temptation, and how sin toyed with eventually becomes our master and overcomes us. 'Satan', Fausset argues, 'like a skilful general, gains by siege many a fort which he could not carry by assault'.[16]

The great snare of hedonism is that it opens the door to the rehabilitation of lust. It is a very small step from pursuing a mystical 'pleasure' in God, devoid of obedience, to seeking pleasure in sin. Herein lies the deadly insidiousness of hedonism: it brings its victims to a ceasefire with the very forces they ought to be vigorously opposing (Mt. 16:18). Once hedonism is embraced, a carelessness enters, defences are relaxed and communication with a wicked world is recommenced. Conversation is restarted around issues which ought not to be named: fornication, homosexuality, and indecent material. The curse of God on the pursuit of evil is preached with less conviction, if at all. Fausset charts the demise of those who embrace this course, one which is now tragically very popular:

> When any ventures so near the edge of ruin, his fall is imminent...
> the spring of [Samson's] strength was his dedication to Jehovah...
> laying down his head in the lap of the temptress, he lost his locks
> of consecration, and with them lost God in him, the only source
> of strength... Lust severs from God, and so reduces the strongest
> to the feeblest... When we lose our godliness, we lose also our
> manliness, for man was made in the image of God.[17]

This tragedy (cf. Lam. 4:7-8) is nowadays all too common. It is too late
when the end is reached, and *mortis rigor* has set in. How much better to
guard against it or indeed challenge the heresy at the time of bewitchment,
as Paul did with the erring Galatians.

Hedonism revives a familiarity with all that Christ is against. Fausset
writes: 'Indifference to evil, easy connivance at its commission, and the
absence of jealous care to clear oneself from complicity in it, are sure marks
of declension in religion'.[18] The Psalmist knew this, hence his fervent prayer
to God (Ps. 139:21-22). By contrast, a familiarity with the Scriptures
strengthens the soul. It is there that one learns of Christ. It is through the
open Book, heeded with a receptive heart, that faith is born, Christ comes
to live in the soul, Christ's love is known, and the fulness of God transforms
the life (Eph. 3:17-19; Rom. 10:17). Therein lay the secret of the success of
the Reformers – their unequivocal return in teaching and conduct to the
infallibility of the Scriptures ensured the exaltation of Christ:

> Every true progress in church history is conditioned by a new
> and deeper study of the Scriptures, which has 'first, second,
> third, infinite draughts'. While the Humanists went back to
> the ancient classics and revived the spirit of Greek and Roman
> paganism, the Reformers went back to the sacred Scriptures
> in the original languages and revived the spirit of apostolic
> Christianity. They were fired by an enthusiasm for the gospel,
> such as had never been known since the days of Paul. Christ
> rose from the tomb of human traditions and preached again His
> words of life and power.[19]

Conclusion

Knowing Christ, in contrast to a slavish pursuit of mysticism, is the only sure precursor to true and lasting joy. For John H. Sammis, the writer of the old hymn 'Trust and Obey' being played in our church hall as I write, obedience preceded joy. First came knowing Christ, then the joy that Christ supplied.

Sammis had his own litany of cares, but he knew Christ. This it was that made all the difference. The second and third of his verses, immortalised by the singing of generations of God's people, reiterate this truth:

> Not a shadow can rise, not a cloud in the skies,
> But His smile quickly drives it away;
> Not a doubt or a fear, not a sigh or a tear,
> Can abide while we trust and obey. […]
> Not a burden we bear, not a sorrow we share,
> But our toil He doth richly repay;
> Not a grief or a loss, not a frown or a cross,
> But is blest if we trust and obey.

Trust and obey Christ, was Sammis' message. Persecution, affliction, burdens, sorrow, grief, loss and toil are to be expected. But these are transient compared to the smile of Christ. Go forth to obey. His blessing will come and your cup will overflow.

The testimony of those who know God is that their obedience has served them well. To delay in service to Christ brings only loss. When counsel comes my way, I must put to death feelings of resentment and self-pity that arise and do what I know to be right. Such obedience I never regret. It was Alfred Lord Tennyson who wrote in his poem on the patriotic charge of 19th century soldiers:

> Theirs not to make reply,
> Theirs not to reason why,
> Theirs but to do and die.
> Into the Valley of Death
> Rode the six hundred.

Tennyson was not prescribing a manual for the discovery of truth – in such circumstances reasoning is to be valued and not condemned. Rather, he was, as Poet Laureate of the United Kingdom, honouring the obedience of the soldiers in the Battle of Balaclava during the unenviable circumstances of the Crimean War. His was a poem to honour simple duty.

The life of the Christian is one of battle, but it is a conflict where victory is already assured. There will often be moments for reflection. However, when we know the truth, and face a life-and-death struggle with sin without or within, there can only be one response of honour and one path to blessing: unquestioning obedience to Christ.

May such a response characterise our lives.

CHAPTER FOUR

SAM ALLBERRY:

TURNING GRACE

INTO

LASCIVIOUSNESS

D URING THE MIDDLE OF THE 20TH CENTURY, HOMOSEXUALITY was a sin which rarely reared its head in public life. However, in less than thirty years, a veritable revolution has occurred. Today almost every country in the Western world recognises same-sex marriage. Openly homosexual politicians hold leading positions in many national governments. Increasingly, homosexuals desire not just special rights but a complete silencing of any who would disagree with their agenda or lifestyle. Universities and schools are becoming more and more inhospitable and even dangerous places for students or staff who communicate their Christian beliefs. Meanwhile, governments all around the world increasingly aggrandise to themselves the power to educate youth in all manner of sexual deviancy, with those who object being vilified and mocked.

Throughout the 80s and 90s in America, Christians opposed the advance of the homosexual agenda at crucial steps. In the closing words of his book *Sodom's Second Coming*, published in 1993, law professor F. LaGard Smith spoke for the faithful when he declared:

> Gay rights is not just another political issue. Nor is it just another moral issue. Gay rights presents us with the ultimate issue of our time: whether or not God will ever again be honoured in our nation. For Christians, the issue is a call to arms.[1]

Thousands of Christians faithfully responded to the call and fought to keep God-honouring laws on the statute books and prevent decadence from being enshrined in law, often fighting vicious battles to achieve successful outcomes. In particular, the battle over Proposition 8 in California in 2008 was a titanic struggle which eventually saw same-sex marriage outlawed:

with turnout at 79%, over 7 million voters (52%) voted to recognise 'only marriage between a man and a woman'.

Over 25 years since LaGard Smith wrote his book, the situation has changed dramatically: in the last decade, in particular, the evangelical church has grown almost silent in its public opposition to homosexuality. To hear a minister or other Christian take a public stand against this vice is a rarity. Public Christian denunciations of the myriad of new pro-homosexual policy initiatives, increasing by the day, are rare. It is almost as if, in many quarters, a truce has been declared between homosexual activists and the professing church.

What has happened to cause this change? This question cannot be answered without a corresponding examination of the men and movements whose popularity has coincided with this decline in faithfulness to God. Having examined Piper's introduction of hedonism to the church, it is worth noting that his popularity has exploded over the last 15 years, particularly with younger people. In June 2009, for example, Piper had approximately 7,000 followers on social media [Twitter]. One year later, this had risen to 70,000 followers. By June 2015, Piper had over 700,000 followers and at the time of writing, this has risen to 1 million. These statistics chart a staggering rise in influence.

The embrace by the church of Piper and his doctrine of hedonism, however, has been paralleled by the embrace of a new doctrine on homosexuality. Piper's Desiring God website has, particularly during the last 10 years, featured material from an array of contributors which does not accord with traditional Christian teaching on homosexuality. Perhaps the most prominent of these 'new voices' is Sam Allberry, a former Anglican priest in the London area who identifies as 'same-sex attracted'. Allberry became increasingly prominent in the evangelical scene following the publication of his book *Is God Anti-Gay?* in 2013, the same year in which he co-founded a new organisation called Living Out.

While Allberry does not credit the doctrine of Piper as the basis for his theology, several of the other 'new voices' on homosexuality have done so. In a 2014 speech at Bethlehem College and Seminary (founded by Piper's church in 2009), one student credited Piper's writing as the incentive for him to go public on his 'same-sex attraction' and stated that there was a counsellor at the seminary who 'specialised in same-sex attraction'.[2] This same individual has written regularly for Desiring God, including critiquing the 'homophobia' within the church.[3] The doctrine of hedonism and the new ideas propounded through Desiring God have clearly served as an impetus to many young people to reconsider the Christian teaching on homosexuality.

The purpose of this chapter is to briefly summarise the main teachings of Sam Allberry as communicated in his book, *Is God Anti-Gay?* Before doing so, it may be helpful to review the traditional message of Christianity on homosexuality:

> (1) homosexual conduct has been and always will be condemned by God (Gen. 19, Lev. 18, Rom. 1),

> (2) while all sins incur the wrath of God, Scripture portrays homosexuality, in particular, as God's giving up of man to lust and a reprobate mind (Rom. 1:24, 26, 28). The Greek word translated here as reprobate is *adokimos* and means unqualified or disqualified, or simply rejected (see 1 Cor. 9:27, Heb. 6:8). It is a sobering word, used in ancient times to describe counterfeit coins or metals. One commentator describes the word as 'speaking graphically of whom God has rejected and left to their own corruption',[4] and

> (3) those who forsake this sin can be forgiven and changed by the power of God (1 Cor. 6:9-11; Isa. 55:7) so that they no longer live in sin.

So, do the teachings of Allberry fit within this biblical framework?

The Paradigm Shift

Perhaps one of the best places to find the core ideas of Allberry's message would be in the mission of the organisation he founded. The three aims of Living Out, as stated on its website, are as follows:

> (1) To help Christian brothers and sisters who experience same-sex attraction stay faithful to Biblical teaching on sexual ethics and flourish at the same time.

> So we've set up this website, speak at churches and conferences, and have written books, to show how you can be same-sex attracted and thrive as a Christian at the same time.

> (2) To help the Christian Church understand how they can better help those who experience same-sex attraction to flourish.

> So we have run training events for Bible college students and existing church leaders to encourage and equip them to build more biblically faithful and compassionate churches where all are encouraged to be more Christ-like regardless of their sexuality and where homophobia is not tolerated.

> (3) To help the wider world hear and understand that there is more than just one viable script for those who are same-sex attracted.

> So we've shared our stories at public events, on-line and via the media to communicate that many same-sex attracted Christians are both happy in their sexuality and the Bible's teaching on same-sex sexual relationships.[5]

The outstanding feature of these aims are their joining together of ideas or teachings which are widely considered to be mutually exclusive. On the one hand, the aims are replete with positive references to Christianity, with phrases such as 'Biblical teaching', 'the Christian Church', and

'Christ-like'. However, every aim of the mission includes the phrase 'same-sex attraction' – calling to mind something which Christians view as forbidden in Scripture and condemned by God. Perhaps the most concerning line, for Christian readers, is the subsection under point 1: the claim to help people 'be same-sex attracted and thrive as a Christian at the same time'.

Many who read these statements are left appalled by the joining of the label 'same-sex attracted' with a claimed allegiance to biblical teaching. The book written by Allberry takes the same approach as Living Out. With this blatant strategy, Allberry and Living Out set out to achieve a *paradigm shift* in the approach of the church to homosexuality: 'a radical change in underlying beliefs or theory'.[6] This paradigm shift can be examined under two headings: a new vocabulary, and a new attitude.

The 'Same-Sex Attracted Christian'

On February 15, 2017, Sam Allberry addressed the Church of England General Synod in London in a speech claiming to support the Christian doctrine on marriage. However, what distinguished his speech were the comments which he made at the outset regarding himself:

> I am same-sex attracted and have been my entire life. By that I mean that I have sexual, romantic, and deep emotional attractions to people of the same sex. I choose to describe myself this way...[7]

Allberry describes himself in the introduction to his book as 'someone who lives with homosexuality'[8] and elsewhere in the book declares 'I battle with homosexual feelings'.[9]

The use of the phrase 'same-sex attracted' by Allberry sets him apart from many in Christian ministry who describe themselves as having left a life of homosexuality. This phrase appears to have been coined by Allberry. In his introduction, Allberry seeks to justify his use of the phrase by claiming that it is different from the use of other words such as 'gay':

> When someone says they're gay... lesbian or bisexual, they
> normally mean that... their sexual preference is one of the
> fundamental ways in which they see themselves. And it's for this
> reason that I tend to avoid using the term. [...] describing myself
> like this [same-sex attracted] is a way for me to recognise that the
> kind of sexual attractions I experience are not fundamental to my
> identity. They are part of what I feel but are not who I am in a
> fundamental sense. I am far more than my sexuality.[10]

In his book, Allberry argues that while 'same-sex attraction is not a good thing' yet he does not believe that to be same-sex attracted, i.e. to be tempted to engage in an impure relationship is itself a sin. This distinction is key, as it gives Allberry sanction to use the phrase in a whole variety of contexts, without any shame:

> Homosexual temptations reflect our own fallenness. But this
> is not the same as saying the presence of temptation itself is a
> sin to be repented of. Christians have always made a distinction
> between temptation and sin. [...] To say that the very experience
> of SSA [same-sex attraction] is a sin seems to suggest that even
> having the capacity to be tempted is itself a sin, something that I
> do not believe Scripture says.[11]

Allberry's insistence on using and popularising the phrase 'same-sex attracted' must be examined carefully as it is central to his message. He uses the phrase widely throughout his book and in his speaking engagements. Before critiquing this phrase, however, it may be useful to consider the importance of language and its power for good or for evil.

The Role of Language

The purpose of language, as discussed in an earlier chapter, is to communicate by calling to mind an object, place, or idea. The King James version of Scripture speaks, in relation to Sodom and Gomorrah, of 'the filthy conversation of the wicked' and how it vexed Lot's soul (2 Pet. 2:7).

While the word *conversation* would be more generally comparable with *conduct* in today's English, there is no doubt that it includes conversation, because the next verse records that Lot's soul was vexed by what he saw and heard. Filthy conversation is when words are used to call evil activities to mind. Such conversation has become part and parcel of the world in which we live, estranged as it is from its Creator.

That Scripture would draw particular attention to the language of Sodom and Gomorrah serves as a reminder that language has a role in legitimising evil. The more a society indulges in evil conversation, the more it serves to legitimise the activities discussed. The wide vocabulary of terms for illicit sexual behaviour popularised in the last half-century have this effect. They call to mind activities and desires which fall into the biblical category of uncleanness. They serve no purpose except to legitimise the activity the more the word is used. Indeed, the use of unchaste language in television comedy shows, arguably, did more to break down society than any rational argument in defence of the indefensible homosexual lifestyle.

The church should always be wary of new language, especially when such language relates to sin or another of the core doctrines of Christianity, for it can serve as a conduit for false doctrine. Evangelist Dave Breese notes how, with the growth of neoorthodoxy after World War II, churches were infiltrated, and churchgoers deceived by the use of time-honoured phrases which had been invested with a new meaning:

> The emphasis they [neo-Orthodox theologians] presented used many words and expressions well known and accepted by believing Christians. The trouble was that they gave these words a new meaning. Consequently, many true believers were deceived into thinking that they were listening to the grand old Christian faith, whereas in reality a new form of spiritual subversion came upon them.[12]

In light of this, the use by Living Out of phrases accepted by many believing Christians, such as 'the Bible's teaching', 'faithful to Scripture' and '[Christian] sexual ethics' should not be taken for granted, but investigated closely. Christians have a responsibility to recognise false prophets by a close examination of their fruits: 'by their fruits ye shall know them' (Mt. 7:20). 'Know' in this context means recognise and recognise with the purpose of avoidance. Is the new vocabulary of Sam Allberry, despite its claim to biblical orthodoxy, faithful to the message of the Scriptures?

A New Vocabulary

Perhaps the most serious error of Allberry's use of the phrase 'same-sex attracted' is that such a phrase is without biblical precedent. Homosexuality in Scripture is never once merely described as a 'temptation' nor are homosexual feelings ever discussed without a link to homosexual conduct. Allberry may find such concepts elsewhere in the realm of psychology but they are alien to Christian theology. Not only so, such concepts are fundamentally at odds with the Christian teaching on conversion and the self-image of the Christian (see "3. Homosexuality and Conversion" on page 100). To link such feelings so closely to a person's persona, so that they become one of their main descriptors, as Allberry does, is antithetical to the teaching of the Scripture.

When it comes to sexual sin in Scripture, it is not the temptation but the actions, secret and open, which are primarily emphasised. The main passage concerning lust in Christ's Sermon on the Mount describes illicit sexual desire in very tangible terms: 'Whosoever looketh on a woman to lust after her hath committed adultery with her already in his heart' (Mt. 7:28). Here Christ describes desire in terms of action – the look of lust is described as committing adultery in the heart – and it is this 'looking' which Christ condemns – a vivid action indeed. The look may be hidden, or even within the realm of the imagination, but it is a choice of the will. There is no discussion here of the temptation to sin but rather the focus is on the sin itself.

Throughout Scripture, emphasis is repeatedly laid on actions and choices of the will rather than 'temptation'. Job declared 'I made a covenant with mine eyes; why then should I think upon a maid?' (Job 31:1) – a clear rejection of wilful sins of the 'eyes' and the 'thinking'. When Joseph was tempted, he boldly declared: 'How then can I do this great wickedness, and sin against God?' (Gen. 39:9). For Joseph, adultery was an unthinkable evil and a sin, ultimately, not against Potiphar but Almighty God. When Christ discussed sin, He warned of the propensity of sinful desire to defile the whole person (Mk. 7:20-23).

Allberry's use of the term 'same-sex attraction' is concerning because of the impression it gives that homosexual feelings are in some way to be excused. In so doing, it undermines the seriousness of sin, and, in particular, the sexual sin which is so rampant in this age. Indeed, as will be discussed in the next chapter, Allberry does not treat homosexuality with any particular opprobrium. Rather, the attitude which Allberry displays towards this sin in his book is somewhat trivial. This is seen, for example, in his chapter on 'Homosexuality and the Christian':

> All of us experience fallen sexual desires, … it is not un-Christian to experience same-sex attraction any more than it is un-Christian to get sick.[13]

At best, this is a gravely misleading statement on the part of Allberry, considering the judgment meted out on sodomy in the Scripture. Homosexuality, in all its forms, is to be shunned by the believer and Scripture is clear that evil desires constitute wickedness (Pr. 21:10). At worst, Allberry's comment is a repudiation of the Christian doctrine of sin. Again, of course, Allberry's use of the verb 'experience' (portraying the Christian as a 'passive' agent in the sentence) and the phrase 'same-sex attraction' cause ambiguity and render his meaning unclear to the average reader.

The concept of 'sexual orientation' has been widely used by the homosexual lobby to legitimise their desires and mollify the public.

Discussing 'temptation' in this fashion, however, treads precipitously close to excusing sin based on the condition of the sinner. This is a diabolical path to tread (Gen. 3:1-5). Those who love the sinner will urge him or her to flee from sin to Christ. In Paul's great letter to the Ephesians, where he urges them to 'walk in love' (Eph. 5:2), his command is immediately followed up with a fulsome rejection of even discussion of sexual immorality. Such discussion is, according to Paul, improper for believers ('as becometh saints' – v3) and out of place ('not convenient' – v4) and he warns in no uncertain terms that an 'unclean person' (v5) incurs the wrath of God and has no 'inheritance in the kingdom of Christ and of God' (v5). Discussion of sinful desire in a spirit of acceptance is forbidden in Scripture, for Paul warns that 'it is a shame even to speak of those things which are done of them in secret' (5:12). Rather, the instruction given is threefold: to avoid partnership (v7, v11), remember past deliverance (v8) and reprove sin (v11) as one seeks what is pleasing to God (v10, v15).

The coining by Allberry of the term 'same-sex attracted' may be considered, by many, a totally legitimate phrase which brings clarity to the issue of homosexuality. One must consider, however, what is being sacrificed for the sake of a perceived 'clarity' – clarity which can only be obtained by a faithful preaching of the Scriptures. Allberry's phrase, with all the ambiguity (not clarity) it introduces, has been received enthusiastically by many professing Christians, who now have just one more excuse not to rebuke sexual sin when they meet it.

Significantly, in the same chapter where Paul warns against sexual immorality, he warns of the power of language to deceive and distract: 'let no man deceive you with vain words' (v6). 'Vain words' are in a modern translation 'empty words' as the Greek word *kenos* (empty) lies behind the translation. Paul warned of words that served no purpose (see 1 Cor. 15:14, where Paul mentions 'vain' preaching or Phil. 2:16, a 'vain' running or labouring). If something is vain it is a waste of time. Paul's warning here is that Christians would be deceived into wasting their time and losing their spiritual sharpness through discussion of things which ought not to be discussed and were contrived to draw them away from Christ. Paul elsewhere warns against Christians being 'spoiled' through 'philosophy and vain deceit' (Col. 2:8). The Greek word here does not mean spoiled as one would use it today, but the sense of 'capturing' somebody in a battle, rendering them useless in service for God. Sadly, this has happened to scores of minds in churches today, particularly those of younger generations.

With this warning in mind, let us turn to the second major concern which the teaching of Allberry raises – its proposal of a new attitude towards 'homosexuals' both inside and outside the church.

A New Attitude

Whatever may be unclear about the intent of Allberry becomes clearer when one examines the new attitude towards 'homosexuals' which he advocates throughout his book. This new approach is perhaps best summarised by a hypothetical situation which Allberry describes in his chapter on the church – the coming of a 'gay couple' into the church and how to respond:

> Sometimes there is the danger of Christians thinking that a gay couple need to be confronted with their sexuality almost the moment they walk through the door; that this needs to be talked about immediately and the couple told what the Bible's teaching is on the whole issue. This is simply not the case.[14]

The advice of Allberry here marks a departure from biblical Christianity on several levels. Firstly, he describes warning somebody of their sinful lifestyle as 'confronting them with their sexuality' – a very ambiguous turn of phrase. Not only so, Allberry explicitly denies any responsibility of the Christian to speedily expose blatant sin where it appears (Eph. 5:11). Lest any reader would be in doubt as to his stance, Allberry continues in defence of his position by saying that should a 'heterosexual couple' who are living in sin arrive in the church, he would not feel obliged to instantly raise with them what he describes as the 'shortcomings' of their lifestyle.

The attitude advocated here shows little regard for the Christian position on the sanctity of marriage and seriousness of sexual sin. Allberry's couching of open sin in terms of 'sexuality' and 'shortcomings' falls short of the biblical standard. John the Baptist did not hesitate to raise Herod's adultery with him but declared 'It is not lawful for thee to have thy brother's wife' (Mk. 6:18). Meeting the woman at the well (Jn. 4:17-18), Jesus raised the subject of her immoral lifestyle in their first encounter. Paul warned the church at Corinth to 'flee fornication' (1 Cor. 6:18), while the writer of Hebrews warned that 'whoremongers and adulterers God will judge' (Heb. 13:4). Allberry, however, says that the issue of living in sin 'doesn't need to be thrashed out for [the couple] to start participating regularly in the life of the church'.[15] This is an affront to Christian teaching.

The attitude of Allberry is one with a light view of sin, and a light view of preaching against sin. In his justification of this approach to homosexuality, Allberry states that 'there is little point in describing how to live in the light of God's grace if someone doesn't yet know God's grace' and that he wants people to [firstly] 'be bowled over by the God of the cross and resurrection'.[16] This is a caricature of true evangelism, however, and a placing of the cart before the horse. Without an awareness of sin, there can be no interest in the cross (Acts 2:37,38; Rom. 3:9). It was Lloyd-Jones who declared: 'Ultimately, the only thing which is going to drive a man to Christ and make him rely upon Christ alone, is a true conviction of sin'.[17]

This minimisation of sin, so to speak, is a feature that appears all throughout Allberry's book. He downplays, for example, the Scripture's condemnation of homosexuality, saying 'there are only a handful of passages in the Bible that directly mention homosexuality...it's just not an issue that comes up' and 'the Bible is not fixated on homosexuality... it is not what the Bible is about'.[18] He speaks of positives in homosexual relationships, saying 'I know gay couples where there is impressive loyalty and commitment'.[19] In one place in the book he resolutely answers the question of the title: 'Is God anti-gay? *No*'.[20]

None of the above statements are in any way close to a Bible stance on the issue of homosexuality. In fact, to embrace the attitude which Allberry advocates towards homosexuality would be to abandon that fear of God and jealously for His holiness which is a characteristic of all who love Him (Heb. 12:14). The Scripture does speak clearly on homosexuality and never treats it as a merely peripheral issue. Those who indulge in the sin of homosexuality are under God's judgment (Rom. 1:18, 26-28) and will incur His condemnation unless they repent (Jude 7).

Is the intent of Allberry to undermine the church's preaching of the Word of God? There is every evidence that this is the case. Some of the harshest words in his book are for Christians who, in his view, offend those caught in homosexuality. This is clear at intervals throughout the book, e.g. when Allberry states that, 'Many Christians still speak about homosexuality in hurtful and pejorative ways',[21] as well as his assertion that 'We must never imply that homosexuality is the sin of our age'.[22] When viewed as a whole, much of the teaching of Allberry involves educating the reader on how to develop a close relationship with homosexuals (in his book he says that conversing with 'those who publicly and proudly self-identify as gay' was a 'privilege').[23] During a 2015 session with the Ethics and Religious Liberty Commission of the Southern Baptist Convention, Allberry talked about the importance of being a 'really good friend' to homosexuals, including asking them 'how long they've been gay'.[24] Allberry said that even if they say they are 'in a relationship... with someone of the same sex', one should say 'well if you're in a relationship I would love to get to know your partner, … a friend of yours is a friend of mine'. Those who followed his advice would no longer prioritise confronting the sinner with their sin.

This new attitude advocated by Allberry is even clearer from a perusal of the advice provided by Living Out, which has as one of its aims, as noted, to make the church a place where 'homophobia is not tolerated'. Living Out goes as far as to advise that a 'same-sex couple' who become Christians could continue to live together with children. When questioned about this and other content on Living Out, Allberry stated at an evangelical conference in Indiana in 2019 that certain articles on Living Out 'should not have been posted' but, at the time of writing a year later, the articles are still available on the website.[25] One can reach no other conclusion but that Allberry and his Living Out organisation have as their mission to subvert the church's faithful preaching of the Word of God and any public stand it might take on the sinfulness of homosexuality.

Conclusion

In Christ's warning regarding false teachers in Matthew 7:15, the first characteristic mentioned is that they will come in sheep's clothing. They will appear to be genuine Christians. Their clothing, i.e. their profession of faith will not give them away. Looking at them, one would never guess that they presented a threat. The activists that Piper has helped introduce to the church, including Sam Allberry, do claim to believe in the inerrancy of Scripture and the sinfulness of homosexual behaviour. However, they are working tirelessly to ensure that the church fully accepts 'gay Christians' and transforms its approach to homosexuality. The church's embrace of their teaching, arguably, represents as serious a departure from biblical Christianity as that which occurred with modernism in the 1920s. The result of this departure can only be a curse (Mt. 7:19).

The fulsome embrace by many of the hedonism of Piper and the teaching of Allberry on homosexuality has unleashed a wave of activists on the church. These activists have one goal: to re-educate the church on homosexuality. They share a common rejection of the Scripture's pronunciation of peculiar shame on homosexual sin and fulsome deliverance for the homosexual from that sin. The black activist Jackie Hill Perry, for example, a regular feature on Desiring God since 2013, is vociferous in her condemnation of those who preach a traditional message on sexual sin. In September 2018, she published an article entitled 'The Heterosexual Gospel' in which the first line stated: 'Stop telling gay people that if they come to Jesus, he will make them straight'.[26] Perry accuses Christians who tell homosexuals they can be completely delivered from their desires as 'preaching another gospel'. Such strident activism is now commonplace, facilitated by the platform provided by John Piper in his Desiring God website.

The effort of such activists to take the church on a guilt trip shows no sign of abating. Rather, their teaching is directed increasingly towards faithful Christians who preach and teach what the Scripture says. If the truth is to be rightly defended, a proper refutation of the errors of Allberry must be on the lips of every Christian.

For none can stand by as grace is turned into lasciviousness.

CHAPTER FIVE

RESCUING GRACE

FROM

LASCIVIOUSNESS

EVERYWHERE IN SCRIPTURE WHERE HOMOSEXUALITY IS MENTIONED IT is roundly condemned. Not only so, spiritual health is closely associated with the rejection of homosexuality. During the spiritual revival under the reign of one godly Israelite king, the Old Testament records that Josiah 'brake down the houses of the sodomites, that were by the house of the LORD' (2 Kings 23:7). Although strictly forbidden under the moral law, homosexuality was pictured here as having returned to Israel during a time of apostasy. Similarly, in the New Testament, Paul warned Timothy in the first chapter of his first epistle of aspiring false teachers and followed it with a reminder of the law's rejection of homosexuality (1 Tim. 1:6-10). While the glories of salvation are a topic for endless blessed discussion (Jude 3), it is necessary at times to turn one's attention to remembering God's judgment on homosexuality (Jude 7, 17-19) and thereby build up oneself.

In Sam Allberry's article at Living Out entitled 'What does the Bible say about homosexuality?' several grossly unscriptural statements are made. Commenting on Romans 1, Allberry states:

> There are no grounds in this passage for singling out homosexual people for any kind of special condemnation.[1]

Allberry later states the following:

> It is important to recognise that Paul is talking here in social rather than individual terms. He is describing what happens to culture as a whole, rather than particular people. The presence of same-sex desire in some of us is not an indication that we've turned from God more than others, but a sign that humanity as a whole has done so.

Later, commenting on 1 Corinthians 6:9-10, Allberry states:

> Homosexual sin is incredibly serious, but it is not alone in being
> so. It is wicked, but so is, say, greed. We must not imply that
> homosexual sex is the sin of the age.

Allberry, in these comments, seeks to shift the blame for his 'same-sex attraction' away from himself to society as a whole. The most glaring errors in these statements are:

(1) Allberry's repeated equating of the sin of homosexuality with other sins,

(2) Allberry's refutation of the individual culpability of those who embrace homosexuality, instead blaming 'culture as a whole', and

(3) Allberry's subtle introduction of the term 'homosexual people' as a particular category of persons.

In response to the last point, it must be said that Allberry preys on the failure of Christians to properly understand the scriptural concept of conversion: the change when one truly comes to Christ and becomes a new creature (2 Cor. 5:17). What follows here is an examination of each of these three errors individually in the light of Scripture.

1. Homosexuality and Other Sins

A hallmark of the message of Allberry is his insistence on an equivalence between homosexuality and other sins. Allberry welcomes the sexual revolution's elevation of homosexuality to a conversational topic, even within the church. In discussion with Albert Mohler, President of the Southern Baptist Convention, and Russell Moore at a conference in 2014, Allberry said:

> I think a lot of things have changed; one of the other things that's
> happened in society with the kind of pro-homosexual message

we're hearing is that it is now okay to talk about it, from a personal point of view, and actually one of the good things that's come from that is that it's easier to talk about the issue personally in church circles. I think that is something we can give thanks for: it's not a taboo...I think that's something we can rejoice in.[2]

Allberry's delight that homosexuality is no longer a taboo, but instead is discussed within the house of God, ought to be an affront to any Christian. The abandonment by Allberry of the clear sexual morality found in Scripture does not stop here, however – he moves on to group homosexuals with other sinners, placing them on equal footing:

> All of us are broken, all of us are sexually broken, all of us have attractions to things which are not what God intended us to have attractions to... there's a sense in which no one is straight. We're all warped and we're all twisted.[3]

The context of Allberry's remarks reveals clearly that his intent is not to argue the universal sinfulness of man, but to insist on an equivalence between homosexuality and other sins. Living Out uses this argument to support welcoming of homosexuals into churches, engagement in regular conversation with proud homosexuals, and, eventually, facilitation of flagrant sexual sin within the walls of one's own home.[4]

Are all sins equally heinous in the sight of God? The framers of the *Westminster Confession of Faith* provided for the church a consideration of this question which has arisen again and again in church history, but perhaps never so often as the present time. The question, number 83 in the well-known *Shorter Catechism*, is answered in a line which breathes conviction:

> Some sins in themselves, and by reason of several aggravations, are more heinous in the sight of God than others.[5]

The blatant nature of homosexuality is testament alone to the seriousness of this sin in the eyes of God. Despite what Allberry may like to believe,

Paul does not select greed as the epitome of rebellion against God. In fact, the sexual degradation of man is pictured here as a root sin of other sins which follow after, including covetousness or greed (Rom. 1:29). It is no surprise that homosexuality is portrayed in Scripture as a very public (v23) and blatant (v27) rejection of God. Referring to the destruction of Sodom and Gomorrah, the 18th century theologian Jonathan Edwards compared God's public judgment on Sodom to the Fall and to Noah's Flood, describing it as the 'liveliest image of hell of any thing that ever had been'.[6]

While Allberry forbids the church to 'imply that homosexual sex is the sin of the age',[7] the Scripture infers here that homosexuality is the sin of the age in any age where it raises its head. Indeed, Allberry's counsel will only deceive those who would be deceived or those who are living 'under a rock' for the forces of evil are working overtime to make sure that homosexuality is the sin of the age. It is no secret that in this generation there has been an aggressive and sustained portrayal of this very sin in the media and the public sphere.

While there is not time here to take a look across the world, a look at my own country will suffice. In Ireland, a country once renowned for its religious constitution and conservative social policies, the 2016 government had two open homosexuals as Ministers, with one of them (Leo Varadkar) subsequently appointed as Prime Minister. The other, the childless homosexual Katherine Zappone (born in Seattle, Washington), who was 'married' to another woman, was appointed Minister for Children, and did untold damage in promoting a secular agenda.

There is no doubt that Zappone's identity as a homosexual is the foundation of her anti-Christian activism. In office, Zappone funded LGBTI+ causes to the tune of hundreds of thousands of euro, weakened parental rights, and subtly eroded freedom of speech with not one but two LGBTI+ strategies in just 3 and a half years. A believer in witchcraft and Wiccan spirituality, Zappone was a primary mover in introducing abortion rights in Ireland and helping overthrow a constitutional ban on abortion that reached back to 1983.

Contrary to what Allberry suggests, Zappone's homosexual identity, Wiccan beliefs, and social activism are not coincidental but deeply interlinked. Homosexuality and social activism go hand in hand. Zappone herself alluded to this repeatedly throughout her political career. In May 2015, speaking in a religious setting in Dublin, Senator Zappone called for the 'dismantling of institutionalised homophobia, transphobia and biphobia'.[8] Lest anyone would be in doubt as to what institution she was targeting, Zappone further explicitly criticised 'laws and systems – fashioned by religious and/or state leaders'. Zappone's goal is to enforce acceptance of homosexuality – and thus rejection of God's Word – on every citizen of the state. Laws, for her, are a vehicle – the means by which society is shaped and her vision of the world advanced. In the same speech, describing her interpretation of the Old Testament term 'Promised Land', Zappone declared, 'the 'Land' that I and many other human rights activists seek is a set of laws, systems, social and environmental conditions'.

Concerned by this attack on Christian mores, I launched a campaign against Zappone's re-election, together with the support of other Christians in early 2020. By means of a detailed website and a ground campaign, we raised awareness of Zappone's hypocritical promotion of the LGBT agenda and hate crime laws while child homelessness soared.[9] Our campaign was successful. Zappone's vote share dropped by 15% and she missed out on her seat at the eleventh count. The homosexual lobby was furious, while Zappone claimed she had lost her seat due to a 'hate-filled campaign against her LGBT activism'. Our campaign had, of course, contained no 'hate' but rather a detailed analysis of Zappone's agenda while in office. Nevertheless, Zappone's only response was to use a favourite weapon of the homosexual lobby: attack the messenger rather than the message.

The parading of evil as virtue calls for a clear response by the people of God and indeed by individual Christians (Mk. 6:18; Acts 17:16). To fail to stand against evil is to disobey our Lord and Master and be punished with those whose sin one ought to have condemned (Jude 23). This is just as true in our age, when homosexuality is paraded as virtuous and wholesome, as it was in the days of the Early Church. Jude put his readers in remembrance of God's judgment on great evils to spur them on to contend for the faith. The three he mentioned were the unbelief of the Israelites, the rebellion of the angels, and the sexual immorality and homosexuality of Sodom and Gomorrah, described as 'giving themselves over to fornication, and going after strange flesh' (Jude 7a). Allberry commands us never to even 'imply that homosexuality is the sin of our age', but Scripture tells us that God has set forth His judgement on this sin as 'an example, suffering the vengeance of eternal fire' (Jude 7b). Could any instruction be more at odds with the clear testimony of Scripture?

Considering the clarity of Scripture on homosexual sin, the argument of Allberry against 'singling out' homosexuality must be firmly rejected. Both the Old Testament and the New Testament *do* single out homosexuality for particular condemnation. Indeed, in both of the two main accounts of homosexuality in the Old Testament, it is portrayed as a more grievous sin than fornication by the main characters involved: Lot in Sodom (Gen. 19:7) and the Levite of Mt. Ephraim in Gibeah (Judg. 19:24). While neither of these men were exemplary models of conduct, the Scripture does record their abhorrence of homosexuality, an abhorrence which Allberry repudiates.

When one examines closely the teaching of Allberry, it becomes clear that his reticence to 'single out' homosexuality is linked with his reinterpretation of the single most significant passage on homosexuality in the New Testament – Romans 1 – and a rejection of individual culpability for this sin. To a close examination of this error and the seriousness of its consequences we now turn.

2. Homosexuality and Individual Responsibility

The first chapter of Romans outlines the degradation to which man sinks outside of God. The main verses under consideration in this section read as follows:

> For this cause God gave them up unto vile affections: for even their women did change the natural use into that which is against nature: and likewise also the men, leaving the natural use of the woman, burned in their lust one toward another; men with men working that which is unseemly, and receiving in themselves that recompense of their error which was meet. (Rom. 1:26-27)

The phrase 'God gave them up' comes from the Greek word *paredōken* and is central to the passage, occurring three times (vv. 24, 26, 28). The word is used regularly in the New Testament for the handing over of a person to judgment or punishment (Mt. 18:34; 27:26; 2 Pet. 2:4). Paul states here that the giving over of men and women to homosexuality is a result of their turning from God (v22) and rejection of His truth (v25).

Allberry, however, rejects this conventional understanding of Romans 1. In his commentary on the verses which mention homosexuality (vv. 26-27), he summarises as follows:

> It is important to recognize that Paul is talking here in social rather than individual terms. He is describing what happens to culture as a whole, rather than particular individuals. The presence of same-sex desire in some of us is not an indication that we've turned from God more than others. But it is a sign that humanity as a whole has done so.[10]

Allberry here denies that Paul is emphasising the individual error of those who embrace homosexuality. According to Allberry, it is 'culture as a whole' that is the focus of Paul and this passage has little or no relevance to the subject of individual responsibility for sin.

Firstly, it must be noted that Allberry here attempts to make Romans 1 refer to 'same-sex desire' rather than the lusts or sinful acts of homosexuality. In his writings elsewhere, Allberry regularly refers to 'same-sex desire' as merely a temptation, describing it as 'homosexual feelings',[11] 'inappropriate attraction toward someone of the same sex',[12] or simply 'same-sex attraction'. However, Paul does not mention temptation at all in this passage. Rather, he speaks of the lusts and acts of homosexuality. This is clearly communicated by the specific words Paul uses in verse 26 – *atimias pathe*, meaning 'vile or shameful passions' – and verse 27 – *aschémosuné*, meaning 'shamefulness' or 'shameful acts'. Paul here portrays the involvement of men and women in homosexuality as a purposeful course of action for which they are responsible.

Secondly, Allberry asserts that God 'gives societies over' to sin rather than individuals. This statement is in conflict, however, with theologians who consider the subject of Paul in Romans 1 to be the indisputable guilt of man before God. The commentator James Barmby, for example, writes:

> [Paul's] whole argument in this chapter involves the doctrine of the *fall* of man, who is conceived to have been originally endowed with Divine instincts, and to have forfeited his prerogative through sin…all men are represented as guilty in that all have sinned against light which they might have followed.[13]

While Barmby speaks of 'the fall of man' and his consequent guilt, Allberry insists that Romans 1 is instead a depiction of the fallenness of society. In one clear example of this, he parallels his 'homosexual feelings' with the presence of suffering in the world:

> There is a parallel with suffering. The presence of particular suffering in someone's life does not mean they've sinned more than someone suffering less. Rather, the presence of suffering anywhere is an indication that as a race we are under God's judgment. Similarly, the presence of homosexual feelings in me reminds me that my desires are not right because the world is not right. Together we have turned from God and together we have been given over to sin.[14]

The trajectory of Allberry here, however, is the complete opposite to that of Paul. The comment of Allberry that his '[homosexual] desires are not right because the world is not right' amounts ultimately to an exoneration of the homosexual and a pointing of the finger at culture, or, dare one say it, at God Himself. The suggestion of Allberry that there is a parallel between suffering, i.e. the sorrow and pain caused by the Fall (Gen. 3:16-19) and 'homosexual feelings' is ill-founded. Sinful desire, Jesus Christ declared, arises from man's heart (Mt. 15:19; cf. Eph. 4:19) and not his circumstances or environment. To find another cause or source for homosexual desires is to make God the author of sin (Jas. 1:13).

Who is responsible?

Against Allberry it must be asserted that *man* is the culprit in Romans 1, not God. Man has every reason to do right but chooses to do wrong. He is ungodly. He is unrighteous. He suppresses the truth (v18). He has every reason to worship his Creator but instead chooses to indulge in the most abominable of deeds. He chooses debauchery and darkness rather than glorifying the immortal God. He is not a victim of his culture – rather, he encourages all he has contact with to defy God also (v32). Romans 1 is the unvarnished portrait of man, guilty before God.

Contrary to the inference of Allberry that 'the world not [being] right' is to blame for his desires, Paul's emphasis is on the *human heart* not being right. This he declares at the very first mention of *paredōken* (giving up): God gave them up to 'uncleanness through the lusts of their own hearts' (v24). Charles Hodge, the Presbyterian theologian, notes that 'the word *kardía*, heart, stands for the whole soul'.[15] Man, his nature corrupted, can look nowhere but *within* for blame. Culture, society, and environment cannot serve as an excuse – indeed, man is 'without excuse' (v20).

Throughout Romans, Paul emphatically presents the doctrine of original sin – that man's positive disposition towards sin originates in the inherited corruption of his heart. This, alone, can explain the debauchery of man described in Romans 1. Robert Haldane, the 18th century Scotsman who, on reading of the French Revolution, resolved to devote himself to the advancement of Christianity, was no less clear about man's condition in his *Commentary on Romans*:

> The impurities into which the Gentiles were plunged, sprung from their own corrupt hearts…The abandonment [*paredōken*] proceeded from Divine justice, but the effect from the corruption of man, in which God had no part.[16]

Ultimately, Romans 1 underscores the guilt of man and vindicates the righteous character of God. Left to the devices of his own heart, the 'free' choices of fallen man lead him further and further down a road of increasing depravity. He, and he alone, is to blame for his sin.

The approach of Allberry to Romans 1 is theologically fraudulent because of what he *refuses* to say. His insistence on using only plural terms is a revival of the modernist tendency, echoed today in scores of pulpits, to speak only in general terms of sin. Congregants are warned of 'dark forces in the world' but never confronted with the sin of their own hearts. This betrayal of Christian doctrine hides from the sinner the only way to salvation – a true conviction of their own sin. It was Louis Berkhof who declared:

> At present many substitute the word 'evil' for 'sin', but this is a poor substitute, for the word 'sin' is far more specific. It denotes a definite kind of evil, namely, a moral evil for which man is responsible and which brings him under a sentence of condemnation.[17]

Like secular psychology, an emphasis only on general evil serves to absolve man from moral culpability and diminish his guilt (the fathers of modern sociology, such as Augustus Comte and Emile Durkheim, viewed all good and evil actions as a product of one's environment). The repentant sinner, however, will not merely speak of 'humanity as a whole' or 'culture as a whole', but will say, 'I have sinned' (Lk. 15:18).

Why homosexuality?

Denying that the theme of Romans 1 is the guilt and debauchery of the human heart, Allberry subsequently downplays the significance of Paul's mention of homosexuality. He argues that the 'giving over' of God is a 'breakdown of human behaviour', a 'long list of antisocial behaviours', and a depiction of how the world has rejected God 'in all sorts of ways'. Allberry speculates that Paul only highlights homosexuality 'because it is a particularly vivid example, or because it was especially pertinent for his readers in Rome given their cultural context'.

There is no need to speculate as to the reason why Paul mentions homosexuality, however. In the first 3 verses of the following chapter, Paul clearly states that it is the specific deeds he mentioned in chapter 1, together with their inevitable judgment, which lie at the heart of his message. Paul mentions homosexuality because of its heinousness in the sight of God. Three times in three verses the phrase 'such things' or 'same things' appears:

> Therefore, thou art inexcusable, O man... for thou that judgest
> doest *the same things*. But we are sure that the judgment of God
> is according to truth against them which commit *such things*. And
> thinkest thou this, O man, that judgest them which do *such things*,
> and doest the same, that thou shalt escape the judgment of God?
> (Rom. 2:1-3, emphasis added)

The word used by Paul for doing in verse three – *poion* - ('O man, that ... doest the same') is associated with the practicing of a pattern of deeds. It is the word used by the Apostle John to contrast those who 'do [or practice] righteousness' or the will of God (2:17, 29; 3:7, 10) with those who 'commit sin' or practice lawlessness (3:4, 8). Those who reject God are given over to a way of life which is characterised by increasing indulgence in sinful thoughts, desires, and deeds (1:26-31).

When Paul speaks of homosexuality in Romans 1, he refers ultimately to a judgment that is meted out on individuals. When Paul speaks of

'God giving them up', the *them* refers to individuals whose sin became their judgment. God granted these individuals a 'longer leash' as it were to sin, and to reap the harvest of sin. Sodom, for example, involved the fulsome participation of individuals: 'The men of the city, even the men of Sodom, compassed the house round, both old and young, *all the people* from every quarter' (Gen. 19:4, emphasis added). The guilt attached to this unnatural vice explains why many homosexual activists are vociferously anti-Christian, leading relentless campaigns to limit religious freedom and influence. Not only so, the corruption of this sin is seen in the egregious medical afflictions which often accompany it, including the chronic scourge of HIV. Paul mentioned homosexuality in Romans 1 because it manifests the perversity of sin and the depravity of the human heart.

The rejection by Allberry of the individual culpability of those ensnared in homosexuality must be seen, then, as a rejection of the plain meaning of Romans 1. This rejection of culpability, however, means that Allberry is also reticent to ascribe a fundamental change to homosexuals after conversion. Indeed, his use of the term 'homosexual Christian'[18] betrays a belief that full gospel deliverance is not really promised to the sinner at conversion. To an examination of this error we now turn.

3. Homosexuality and Conversion

Conversion, in Christian theology, means change. The house in which I was raised during my childhood years was totally changed following our arrival. Set on approximately two acres, the oblong bungalow and large shed adjoining the house were transformed beyond all recognition over the space of about ten years. An extension was added to the house, paint to the walls, and flowers, hedging and plants to the garden. Colour replaced drabness and order supplanted chaos. On the wall in our hallway hung for many years an aerial photo of the house taken from a plane. The photo served as a poignant reminder of the reality of change, and how the passage of time can mean great change for the better.

Why the change? The answer is simple: a new owner. New ownership in the Christian life, the ownership of God (1 Cor. 6:19-20), means transformation, just as new ownership transforms a property. The 'old…[is] passed away; all…[is] become new' (2 Cor. 5:17). Perhaps this is why conversion is so often captured in the hymns of the church, where conversion is indissolubly linked with glorious change: whether Newton's 'Amazing Grace', Wesley's 'Long My Imprisoned Spirit Lay', or Crosby's 'I Am Redeemed'.

Throughout the writings of Allberry is littered a clear attempt to wed homosexuality to the Christian life, insofar as to deny a deep change at conversion. This denial is a clear renunciation of the doctrine of conversion. Conversion has two elements: repentance and faith. The word conversion means *turning* – from sin to Christ. This is a momentous change and summarises the sinner's response to the effectual gospel call. Notably, the Old Testament commanded that the 'wicked forsake his way, and the unrighteous man his thoughts' (Isa. 55:7), illustrating the breadth of repentance and how it encompasses even the innermost thoughts of the mind.

To deny the homosexual deliverance from his sin is not just to deny the reality of conversion, it is to deny the efficacy of the atonement. If a convert is 'yet in his sins' (1 Cor. 15:17), the atonement has no practical power to liberate the sinner from sin. Christ died to deliver the sinner from sin (Mt. 1:21) and in His earthly ministry consistently pinpointed the most pressing sin of the individual with which He conversed. To continue in sin or make a practise of sinning was unthinkable, for Christ came to 'destroy the works of the devil' (1 Jn. 3:8-10).

With the Protestant Reformation came a renewed emphasis upon the efficacy of the blood of Christ, in opposition to Rome's denial of the finality of the sacrifice of Christ. The consequence of Rome's denial is, as Boettner says, 'that sins are really never taken away and that those who are called priests pretend to continue the unfinished work of Christ'.[19] This, of course, is blasphemy. Christ's sacrifice was 'fully efficacious and complete for the accomplishing of what He intended'.[20] The sinner can be delivered from his sin. The blood of Christ, the scriptural motif for the death of Christ in its saving aspects, is associated particularly with victory over the power of sin (1 Jn. 1:7; Rev. 1:5b), conquering of the devil (Rev. 12:10-11), and deliverance from a sinful way of life (1 Pet. 1:18-19). While there is of course a battle in the Christian life with indwelling sin, those who know nothing of the power of the blood cannot be heirs of God (Rom. 8:17).

The stance of Allberry, however, is also a blasphemy against the doctrine of the atonement. His book lays no emphasis on the blood of Christ, or joy in the power of the blood to cleanse from sin. In fact, Allberry's view of homosexuality and the Christian is almost identical to that of Rome, which has tolerated homosexual desires in its clergy for generations and whose church documents manifest an ambivalence towards homosexual identity.[21] This, of course, is little surprise as their doctrinal rejection of the blood of Christ is a rejection of the power of the cross to grant victory over indwelling sin. The teaching of Allberry, then, is simply a revival of Roman Catholic doctrine.

Does the Christian experience any tension, then, in his everyday life? Of course, a battle with indwelling sin is to be expected (Heb. 12:1). However, the believer is not, as Rome and Allberry argue, locked in chains of sin. Rather, the Christian is indwelt by the Holy Spirit and avails of the power of the Spirit to resist sin (Rom. 8:9-11). The believer is not at the mercy of his sins, rather he is dead to his sin in Christ. Yes, he has not been completely liberated from sin; but the song of victory is on his lips. He is like the Allied soldiers who fought between D-Day (6 June 1944), when the Allies successfully returned to the Normandy beaches, and V-E Day (8 May 1945) when Nazi Germany surrendered.[22] Between both these days, the victory of the Allies was a good as certain, their enemy as good as dead, but the end had not yet come.

This state is portrayed in the New Testament in vivid terms as the battle between the 'old man' and the 'new man'. The two major passages in Scripture which deal with this battle are Ephesians 4 and Colossians 3. Significantly, both passages begin with exhortations against sexual sin: Ephesians the 'lasciviousness…[and] uncleanness' (Eph. 4:19) of other Gentiles, and

Colossians the 'fornication [and] uncleanness' of the 'children of disobedience' (Col. 3:5). These words convey sexual immorality in all its sensuality and impurity, including homosexuality. The Christian is urged to utterly and totally break from such sins, associated with his past life, and live in the new power of the Christian life.

Anthony Hoekema, a skilled Reformed theologian of the 20th century, wrote many books, one of which is entitled: *The Christian Looks at Himself.* In this short but effective book, he examines the scriptural interpretation of the tension which the Bible presents as existing between the old man and the new man. While activists such as Allberry advocate a very polarised view of the Christian life, and one in which the temptation to sin ('same-sex attracted') looms as large or larger than the power to overcome sin, Hoekema definitively rejects this proposition. In his chapter entitled 'Old and New Man', Hoekema says:

> The old and the new man, it seems to me, ought not to be seen as aspects or sides or parts of the believer which are both still somehow present in him. [..] What happened when Christ was crucified has also been subjectively appropriated by us.[23]

Hoekema then goes on to expound Paul's commands in Ephesians 4:22-24 and Colossians 3:9-10 regarding putting off the old man and putting on the new. He declares regarding the latter:

> In this passage, therefore, Paul appeals to his readers not to lie to each other because they have once and for all put off the old man or old self and have once and for all put on the new man or the new self. Our self-image as Christians, therefore, must be of ourselves as those who have decisively rejected the old self or old man (the total person enslaved by sin), and have just as decisively appropriated the new self or the new man (the total person ruled by the Spirit)... We are to see ourselves, therefore, not as partly old selves and partly new selves, but as new persons in Christ.[24]

This clear depiction of how the Christian should view himself raises problems for Allberry. If the Christian is to have a self-image of one who is completely delivered from the power of sin, then to appendage a label to one's identity such as 'same-sex attracted' ultimately excuses a desire to sin. Hoekema emphasises the totality of the Christian's break with the past: he has 'decisively rejected' and 'once and for all' put off the old man. The hankering of Allberry for a crutch which links him with his sin amounts to a rejection of Christian doctrine.

The Christian is not to consider himself half old man and half new man. While Hoekema acknowledges that the Christian will wrestle with temptation, he does not capitulate on his main point:

> [This] does not mean that we must therefore revise our self-image as having to include both old man and new man. For – and this is a most important point – when we slip into an old-man way of living, we are living contrary to our true selves; we are denying our true self-image. Paul does not say in Romans 6:11, 'Consider yourselves to be mostly alive to God and mostly dead to sin'. What he says is, 'Consider yourselves dead to sin and alive to God'. This, then must be our Christian self-image. We must consider ourselves to be new persons in Christ, who have once and for all turned our backs upon the old self, and who therefore refuse to be identified with it any longer.[25]

Hoekema pinpoints here the heart of the matter: what the Christian's self-image should be. The Scripture does not present this as a matter of individual choice for the believer, but instead as a command to be obeyed: 'consider yourself'. Both the Ephesians and the Colossians passages also instruct that the key to battling sin is a renewal of the mind. To be 'renewed in the spirit of your mind' (Eph. 4:23; Rom. 12:2) is to saturate one's mind with knowledge of one's new identity in Christ (Col. 3:10). Prayerful meditation on God's Word (Ps. 119:11) is the only sure defence against temptation (Ps. 119:9). Here is the way of strength, of purity of conscience, and of a Christian testimony described by David as 'the undefiled' who 'do no iniquity' (Ps. 119:1-3).

Hoekema's very faithful interpretation of, not just this passage of Scripture, but the whole subject of the believer's identity in Christ excludes utterly the possibility of a Christian referring to himself with a sin-attracted label. It condemns in the strongest possible terms Sam Allberry's attempt to revise the image of the Christian to include both the old man and the new man. The use by Allberry of the phrase 'same-sex attracted' calls sin, and gross sin at that, to the minds of all who hear it – believers or unbelievers. Significantly, were a believer to accept the teachings of Allberry, he would still be identifying himself by his former sin, in contrast to Hoekema who says that a true believer ought to 'refuse to be identified with it any longer'.[26]

Hoekema, in his short book, never relents on the fact that Christians must view themselves as new creatures in Christ, without exception and without reserve. Yes, temptation will come, but this temptation does not define us, but rather our faith in Christ. 'As those who have that faith', Hoekema says, 'we must see ourselves not as victims but as victors....we who are in Christ are to view ourselves as new creatures who are now in the strength of the Spirit living a life of victory'.[27]

This is wholesome advice: good, righteous, and true. Christians are not victims of hedonism and homosexuality but victors in Christ. One can only conclude that those who reject this advice are not truly made new in Christ but are clinging fast to sins from which they have never been delivered.

The Gospel for the Whole Person

Throughout the history of Christianity, there has been ebb and flow; but Christianity has always been strongest at those times when truth changed personalities, i.e. when truth was brought to bear on the whole man.[28] This it was that shook towns, nations and the world in the providence of God. This is true Christianity – not the form of religion, but the vitality of a faith that turns men and then the world 'upside down' (Acts 17:6). The revival of

England under the Wesley brothers was no accident, but born of a return to a living faith, birthed in the heart of Susannah Wesley, their mother, who reputedly said: 'There are two things to do about the gospel: believe it and behave it'.[29] Today a distorted faith is in vogue, popularised by Allberry and Piper, where a false 'believing' takes precedence over behaving or, in some cases, has supplanted it altogether. True faith, however, balances a love for doctrine with a life of good works.

Great men of God have taken pains to emphasise this in their preaching and teaching, with a holy reverence for God seldom seen in today's pulpiteers. The gospel, truly preached, is preached to engage man's mind as a precursor to inflaming his heart and transforming his will. Robert Murray M'Cheyne, the Scottish minister who died before his 30th birthday, declared that 'a holy man is a mighty weapon in the hands of God' and 19th century Scotland felt the influence of his full gospel.

A faithful church and minister must preach salvation in its fulness. Allberry and Piper preach a message which is easily received because it can be embraced without a fulsome repentance of sin. Scripture's teaching on the washing of the sinner that accompanies conversion is subverted (Titus 3:5). The homosexual remains a homosexual. The regenerating power of the gospel to convince the conscience, prick the heart and renew the will is denied. It was Martyn Lloyd-Jones who, in his sermon on Romans 6:17 declared regarding the gospel:

> It can satisfy man's mind completely, it can move his heart entirely, and it can lead to wholehearted obedience in the realm of the will. That is the gospel. Christ has died that we might be complete men, not merely that parts of us may be saved; not that we might be lop-sided Christians, but that there may be a balanced finality about us.[30]

Lloyd-Jones was in no doubt that salvation was an experience that fundamentally changed mind, heart and will, and not one at the expense or to the exclusion of the others. By contrast, the gospel of Sam Allberry and John

Piper does not leave their hearers merely lop-sided: it leaves them still in their sins (1 Cor. 15:17). This might indeed be a religion, but it is not Christianity. Preaching on the mind, the heart, and the will, Lloyd-Jones declared:

> The Christian position is threefold; it is the three together, and the three at the same time, and the three always. A great gospel like this takes up the whole man, and if the whole man is not taken up, think again as to where you stand. 'You have obeyed from the heart the form of doctrine delivered unto you'. What a gospel! What a glorious message![31]

Lloyd-Jones, a Welsh minister with years of experience in practical ministry, knew well the dangers of doctrine which emphasised one aspect of man's personality over another. It is little surprise that in the conclusion to his sermon, he singled out the emotions as an area of particular concern. Those who follow the emotive teaching of Piper would do well to heed his warning:

> I have known evil-living men to find false comfort, to their own damnation, in the fact that they could still weep and be moved emotionally in a religious meeting. 'I cannot be all bad or else I would not respond like this', they have argued. But it is a false deduction – their emotional response was produced by themselves. Had it been a response to Truth their lives would have been changed.[32]

Lloyd-Jones' sobering words from over fifty years ago ring true in our ears today. To be merely 'moved emotionally' will only incur damnation. A response to truth shows itself in a changed life. Unless our religion teaches us to forsake lasciviousness, we are denying God (Jude 4). Let us heed the preacher's call to examine ourselves, soberly analyse our deepest beliefs, and let Scripture be our only guide.

CHAPTER 6

HOLINESS

NOT

HEDONISM

FOR OVER TWO DECADES, JOHN PIPER HAS SPOKEN at an annual conference for young people between 18 and 25. Passion Conference is held in Atlanta, Georgia, and attracts approximately 50,000 young people every year. Piper has been a regular keynote speaker at the conference, including at the inaugural conference in 1997, and customarily uses the event to preach his doctrine of hedonism. During the 2020 Passion Conference, the music, as usual, featured various bands playing raucous music, as the crowd raved under strobe lights. One set of lyrics included the following lines:[1]

> He's [God is] alright with your past
> He's not mad with any one of us
> But He waits with open arms
> […]
> He's not moved by perfection
> Or how well we look the part
> But He's wild about the hidden stuff
> Like He's wild about the heart.

The Passion Conference 'worship' is grossly irreverent, with the above lyrics betraying a view of God as a chum or pal, and One no longer to be feared. The behaviour of the audience indicates that they have become like that which they really worship – the world – with little or nothing to distinguish the atmosphere from that of a rock concert. The music of Passion is characterised by an exaltation of self and an absence of scriptural truth.

The teaching of Passion is no different: at Passion 2020, one keynote speaker, Christine Caine, listed the great evils of the day as racism, sexism, misogyny, legalism, religion, judgment, and condemnation.[2] However, this is a list with which, in all likelihood, the average young person of our day would agree. Marxism, the atheistic philosophy of life which undergirds much modern social discourse, proclaims the source of all evil to be, not sin, but the 'dominion of the bourgeoisie [the "haves"] over the proletariat [the "have nots"]'.[3] Marxism has taken over Western schools and universities and is being championed in the media, not to mention through organisations such as Black Lives Matter (whose co-founder, Patrisse Cullors has declared herself and another co-founder to be 'trained Marxists').[4] Caine surely knows this and is proclaiming a message which dovetails with the culture of the day. Her hierarchy of evils fits neatly into the Marxist dialectic which, redefining good and evil, has changed the meaning of sin 'from rebellion against God into striving for individual ends as opposed to the collective'.[5]

However, as Paul warned the Corinthians, there can be no concord between Christ and Belial (2 Cor. 6:15). Karl Marx was clear about his aim – 'My object in life is to dethrone God and destroy capitalism' – and all who join hands with Marxist ideologues reject the God of the Scriptures. When one embraces the world's hedonism, one also embraces an affinity of morals. Christianity becomes squeezed into the mould of the world, and the Scripture's absolutes on sin, condemnation and redemption are supplanted by the world's changing explanations for its own chaos and disorder. It is little surprise that Passion is shallow in commitment, seriousness, and depth about biblical truth, for only by godly reverence comes genuine consecration.

The writer of Hebrews, as he approached the end of his letter, spoke of only one indispensable virtue without which no one would see God: holiness (Heb. 12:14). Christ warned that entering into God's kingdom was predicated on doing God's will, and that mere words and profession counted for nothing: 'Not everyone that saith unto me Lord, Lord, shall enter into the kingdom of heaven; but he that doeth the will of my

Father which is in heaven' (Mt. 7:21). Those who follow the teaching of Allberry and Piper depart from doing God's will. Faced with the sin of homosexuality and its rampant promotion in our secular society, they refuse to rebuke it wholeheartedly. The unpopular rebuking, reproving and exhorting of Scripture (2 Tim. 4:2) are replaced with a false formula for pleasing God.

The modernists of the 1920s undermined truth by denying the plenary, verbal inspiration of an inerrant Bible. The hedonists of the 2020s, the protégés of Piper, undermine the proclamation of truth – faithful preaching and a full declaration of all that the Scriptures say. The teaching of Piper and Allberry reduces the church to a place where it no longer speaks clearly on sexual sin. As a result, the church is weakened just as effectively as if it had succumbed to the struggle of the 1920s, for the preaching and teaching of God's truth are central to the faith (2 Tim. 4:2; Mt. 28:20). And, 'if the foundations be destroyed, what can the righteous do?' (Ps. 11:3).

Many may ask, where does such a slippery slope end? Where does a refusal to condemn what God has condemned eventually take the avid follower of this false doctrine? Can one simultaneously claim adherence to Scripture while eschewing the contention for the faith which the Scripture so solemnly commands? Or like a slow poison, will the dangers of such a paradox only be seen when it is too late?

The Lord Jesus Christ answers this question in Matthew 7 by means of a metaphor. Those who heard His instruction and did it, He compared to a well-built house with a good foundation which could withstand adverse weather. When this house was tested, 'it fell not: for it was founded upon a rock' (Mt. 7:25). It is difficult to think of a more apt metaphor of stability, strength, and resilience. Those who heard His words but did not do them, Christ compared to a house built on sand. No doubt such a house would have looked well at first, but with the passage of time, and the advent of adverse rain, floods and wind, 'it fell, and great was the fall of it' (Mt. 7:27).

The Stand of Holiness

A resolute refusal to conform to worldly fashions has long been one of the distinctive hallmarks of real Christianity (Rom. 12:2). This holy distinctiveness is the practical manifestation of an inner purity. Those who belong to Christ, Paul notes, have 'crucified the flesh with the affections and lusts' (Gal. 5:24). The use of the word crucifixion here denotes a bitter death struggle in which lust is once and for all revoked. This sign of those who are Christ's is not a doctrine on paper, but a living reality of daily life.

The Fundamentalist-Modernist controversy in the Presbyterian Church in the United States from the 1920s onwards provides a clear illustration of this insistence on practical Christianity. The Fundamentalists' allegiance to the cardinal doctrines of Christian orthodoxy was paralleled by a strong commitment to practical holiness of life. One example was the early repudiation of social dancing by many Fundamentalist churches. Clarence E. Macartney, a minister in Pennsylvania during this time, exemplified this stance. Described as the Fundamentalist Prince of the Pulpit, Macartney was the man who famously responded to the modernist Harry E. Fosdick's sermon 'Shall the Fundamentalists Win?' with the sermon 'Shall Unbelief Win?' The late minister and Boston University professor C. Allyn Russell notes concerning Macartney:

> [Macartney] was not hesitant to condemn specific evils...he spoke against dancing, drinking, the cinema, the comic sheet, sexual irregularities, prizefighting, birth control, and the desecration of the Sabbath. Macartney saw dancing as death to the spiritual life of both individuals and congregations.[6]

Macartney's aversion to even the slightest hint of immorality demands serious reflection. This preacher was in no doubt that the dance was a tool of the devil to kill spiritual desires and inflame the worst instincts of the flesh. He viewed the dance, with its entanglement with sexual immorality, as paralysing not just individual spirituality but the collective welfare of God's people. For Macartney, its sinister effect on spiritual life was palpable.

For the church during this period of crisis, truth was just as much personal and practical as it was doctrinal. Russell notes that while Macartney's 'customary methods of opposition to personal iniquities were his pulpit pronouncements and his books',[7] he did not hide behind the pulpit. By his practical life, he set the laymen and laywomen of Pittsburgh and Philadelphia an example. Russell records that Macartney's Christianity extended to his visiting the state legislature as bills were discussed and walking through the cities where he laboured to counter the rampant vice.[8] Should any think that Macartney's religion was one of works, his declaration as he began ministry in Pittsburgh is clear: 'I have no theological knickknacks, novelties or sensations, but a profound and experimental faith in the power of the gospel'.[9]

The testimony of Macartney is a vivid example of the strength which ought to characterise those who name the name of Christ. His generation was in no doubt that a claim to follow Christ without obedience to His Word was of no value whatsoever. Rather, faith was seen in works of obedience which, imbued with holy energy, staved off the compromise of modernism and led to the establishment of new schools, churches and seminaries. This uncompromising spirit, rewarded by God, was summarised by Macartney's comrade J. Gresham Machen, who in 1920 declared in his book *Christianity and Liberalism*: 'The present is a time not for ease or pleasure, but for earnest and prayerful work'.[10]

The Fall of Hedonism

In contrast to Macartney and Machen, our generation is characterised by a compromised Christianity bereft of spiritual strength. Rather than bringing strength to the church, the scandals wreaked by false teachers have brought great disrepute on the name of Christ. One example is the blasphemous mega-pastor Mark Driscoll, who fell from favour in 2014 following multiple allegations of misconduct. Driscoll's church network, with an attendance of over 12,000 in 2013, was dissolved within 3 months of his resignation.

John Piper mentored Driscoll for many years, including inviting him to speak at his Desiring God Conference several times. Approximately a year after Driscoll's fall, Piper gave an interview, posted on the Desiring God channel, where he discussed the saga.[11] Here Piper acknowledged that Driscoll named him as a mentor, but there was no horror at the shame caused to the church or repentance for the role which Piper had played in the devastation. Rather, Piper breezed through the interview, laughing and smiling along the way. He praised Driscoll's preaching and downplayed the gross disrepute to religion that the situation had caused. Piper quipped that 'Christians are failing every day and bringing reproach upon the gospel' and compared Driscoll's gross sin to a Christian doing something out of character at the office. In responding to Driscoll's demise, Piper advised that Christians should be 'slow to judge', quoting Matthew 7:3. Looking at the overall scheme of events, Piper argued that God uses 'defective' ministries (Phil. 1:15-18) and described the Driscoll incident glibly as a 'tactical defeat'.

Piper's response was everything one should expect from a false teacher: trite, disingenuous, and a refusal to deal with the root cause of Driscoll's disgrace (Mt. 7:27). His one concern seemed to be to limit the fallout which Driscoll's desperate reputation and exposure might have had for his own influence, appealing to people not to give up on 'Reformed theology, complementarianism or the church'. There was no remorse for sin.

Another formerly close associate of John Piper is Joshua Harris. Harris is a published author whose 1997 book, *I've Kissed Dating Goodbye,* sold over 1.2 million copies. In 2013, he was featured on Piper's website with the Piper-inspired video message 'Don't waste your sexuality'.[12] He shared a stage with Piper and his many books were regularly reviewed and promoted by Piper. Indeed, one of his latest books was said to have come from a conversation he had with Piper, a book which focused on people not exhibiting an 'arrogant orthodoxy' but instead learning how to 'hold the truth high without putting people down'.[13] It was clear that this individual had wholeheartedly embraced the ideology at the heart of hedonism – change the church by changing the church's historic presentation of the truth.

In July 2019, Harris announced that he had renounced his faith and was no longer a Christian. Notably, Harris said that he wanted to apologise to the 'LGBTQ+ community' and posted on Instagram: 'I regret standing against marriage equality, for not affirming you and your place in the church, and for any ways that my writing and speaking contributed to a culture of exclusion and bigotry. I hope you can forgive me'. A few days later, Harris posted photos of himself marching in the Vancouver Pride Parade and sharing photos with LGBT activists.

Today's 'celebrity pastors' stand in stark contrast to the lives and testimonies of holy men of God in times past. The latter did the will of God, rather than dabble in words, psychology, and philosophy. Their holy lives spoke for God, preaching righteousness in days of iniquity and lawlessness, and as they grew older, their testimonies became stronger, for their Christian lives were 'founded upon a rock' (Mt. 7:24). They did not crumble before the giants of secular and pagan culture, but instead stood tall, impervious to persecution. Their courage rose with the danger of the hour – the spirit of Polycarp who, threatened with wild beasts by the Roman proconsul Statius Quadratus, responded in faith-filled courage: 'Call for them'.[14]

The Essential Chastity

The Scripture tells us why the Christian sexual ethic is particularly hated by the world: homosexuality is a rejection of God's natural order (Rom. 1:28). It is a sign of man's fallen nature and his fateful decision to 'worship and serve the creature rather than the Creator' (Rom. 1:25). The Apostle John reminds us that sensuality and love for God are so far apart as to be mutually exclusive: 'If any man love the world, the love of the

Father is not in him. For all that is in the world, the lust of the flesh, and the lust of the eyes, and the pride of life, is not of the Father but is of the world' (1 John 2:15b-16).

It is no surprise that the most virulently atheistic of 19th century philosophers were deeply consumed by sexual matters, including Friedrich Nietzsche and his disciple Sigmund Freud. Freud, the Austrian neurologist who died of overdoses of morphine, sought to place the drive for sexual pleasure at the core of human development. His influential work only serves to illustrate the absurd and unreasonable value which those who deny God place on the hedonistic pursuit of pleasure. Freud's unrelenting animosity towards Christian morality illustrates the twofold influence of Christian teaching: 'to the one we are the savour of death unto death; and to the other the savour of life unto life' (2 Cor. 2:16).

There is a word rarely heard in today's conversation, but one which Scripture uses as a description of the Christian: the word *chaste*. Chaste means 'refraining from immorality' or 'free from obscenity' and in English comes from the Latin word *castus* which means 'clean' or 'pure'. The Greek word of the New Testament text, *hagnos*, is often translated pure in modern paraphrases, but has the deeper meaning of pure inside and out. It is perhaps one of the strongest words in biblical Greek to describe a deep, pervading purity, which reaches 'to the centre of one's being'.[15]

The word *chaste*, far from indicating a superficial acquaintance with God's law, describes a person who is a living example of closeness to God, loving what God loves and hating what God hates. Indeed, the very word *hagnos* originates from the same root as the word 'holy' (*hagios*), the only attribute of God appearing in triplet form in Scripture (Isa. 6:3; Rev. 4:8).

The word *chaste* (Greek *hagnos*) only appears three times in the New Testament. The first is where Paul uses the word to describe his responsibility to God regarding the church, i.e. to present her as a 'chaste virgin to Christ' (2 Cor. 11:2). Paul chides the Corinthians in the same letter for bearing with those who brought a different gospel, a gospel leading to impurity, fornication and lasciviousness in the congregation (2 Cor. 12:21).

The other two appearances of the word *chaste* in Scripture appear in the context of expectations for Christian conduct. In Titus 2, we read of Paul's instruction to Titus. Notably, the focus of Paul was not solely on doctrine, but also on what 'became' or accorded with sound doctrine, i.e. the practical holiness of life that fitted with his teaching. Part of this instruction was that young women be 'chaste...that the word of God be not blasphemed' (Titus 1:15). For Paul, to preach doctrine but devalue holiness of life amounted to blasphemy of God's Word. This sober warning has relevance to all churches which have inherited a legacy of doctrinal orthodoxy but are unfaithful in disciplining a younger generation enmeshed in sinful lifestyles.

Finally, the Apostle Peter used the word when speaking directly to wives in the church. Peter here deals with the effect of a chaste life on those outside the church: 'that, if any obey not the word, they also may without the word be won by the conversation of the wives; while they behold your chaste conversation coupled with fear' (1 Pet. 3:2). Although Peter advocated a ready defence of the faith (1 Pet. 3:15), his use of this word suggests that there are times when preaching alone is inadequate to conquer the human heart. In such situations, what could convince where words failed was chaste conduct. Purity of life, genuine, sincere purity, could win 'without the word' or, as can be translated, 'without a word'.

Resisting the Conspiracy of Silence

Knowing God, then, is not something that is evidenced in self-satisfaction or a mystic spirituality. Rather, Daniel 11:32 reminds us that true knowledge of God reveals itself in action: 'the people that do know their God shall be strong and do exploits'. There is no room in Christendom for those who desire an easy life, or for those whose preference it is to sit out the battle with principalities and powers 'on the fence'. Scripture divides the inhabitants of the earth with a simple dichotomy: 'They that forsake the law praise the wicked: but such as keep the law contend with them' (Pr. 28:4). Boldness in Christian service to take on the forces of hell (Eph. 6) should be the aspiration of every child of God.

Today, the inhabitants of Sodom, i.e. those that share the same interests as the men of that ancient city, are literally marching. The homosexual lobby realise fully that they are in a battle to influence the nation. Hence, their pride marches – public, intimidating, highly visible expression of pride in what Scripture says is a 'dishonourable' and 'unseemly' sin (Rom. 1:24, 27) – are carefully orchestrated to cause maximum impact. Pride marchers are not merely 'enjoying themselves' – they realise they are in a battle for minds and they are doing their best to win it.

When Christ was on earth, however, He depicted *the church of God* as marching in attack against the gates of hell (Mt. 16:18). What a tragedy that, due to the proliferation of false doctrine, many pulpits now preach compromise with all that Christ is against. Few are the voices raised in defence of a holy faith. Instead, the insidious teachings of John Piper and Sam Allberry are permitted to circulate unchallenged and undermine the doctrines of truth. Those who would shake hell are becoming increasingly voices in the wind, while a vast majority of churchgoers refuse to stand against evil.

In 1887, the Baptist Union of Great Britain faced a battle within its own ranks known as the 'Downgrade Controversy'. The English preacher Charles Spurgeon described the fight as one involving both modernism and worldliness. Writing in his magazine *The Sword and the Trowel*, he described the culprits as Baptist ministers who 'scouted the atonement [and] derided the inspiration of Scripture' as well as endeavouring to 'unite church and stage, cards and prayer, dancing and sacraments'.[16] However, his choicest words were for those Baptist church members who were claiming to be evangelical but whose voices were strangely silent:

> Little as they [faithful Baptists] might be able to do, they could
> at least protest, and as far as possible free themselves of that
> complicity which will be involved in a conspiracy of silence. If
> for a while the evangelicals are doomed to go down, let them
> die fighting, and in the full assurance that their gospel will have
> a resurrection when the inventions of 'modern thought' shall be
> burned up with fire unquenchable.[17]

To protest the error of the day, as Spurgeon knew, is not an option for
those faithful to Christ, nor is it a great ask. It is but a 'little' service which
marks one out as in no way joined to those who forsake God's Word,
but rather contending against them. The only other option, in Spurgeon's
eyes, was to be 'complicit' (i.e. an accomplice in crime) in the heresies of
the day, betrayed by one's silence. The temporal cost of a faithful stand
did not bother Spurgeon, for he knew that he would be vindicated in the
judgment of the final day.

In the face of rampant cultural immorality, and the infiltration into the
church of activists who have made Christ the 'minster of sin' (Gal. 2:17),
the church must reclaim its holy calling. Chastity of life must once more
become the spotless garment of the people of God, condemning the
vulgarity of rebellion against God and winning those who are impervious
to a bare profession. Men of the calibre of Charles E. Macartney can
once again call the church to its great and holy heritage, by, like him,
condemning without hesitation the specific evils of their day. Such
Christians will know the Word of God, walk in its doctrines, and faithfully
proclaim its precepts without compromise.

The 19th century American poet Josiah Gilbert Holland made the
appearance of such men his prayer. It is reproduced below, a sober call to
God's people to live above the fog of the age, repossess the virtue of true
Christianity and, for the sake of God and man, live up to the glorious
heritage of Christian duty.

GOD, give us men! A time like this demands

Strong minds, great hearts, true faith and ready hands;

Men whom the lust of office does not kill;

Men whom the spoils of office can not buy;

Men who possess opinions and a will;

Men who have honor; men who will not lie;

Men who can stand before a demagogue

And damn his treacherous flatteries without winking!

Tall men, sun-crowned, who live above the fog

In public duty, and in private thinking;

For while the rabble, with their thumb-worn creeds,

Their large professions and their little deeds,

Mingle in selfish strife, lo! Freedom weeps,

Wrong rules the land and waiting Justice sleeps.[18]

God, give us such!

CHAPTER SEVEN

TAKING A LOOK

AT OURSELVES

SØREN KIERKEGAARD, THE DANISH PHILOSOPHER OF THE 19TH century, declared regarding the church: 'Take away the alarmed conscience and you may close the churches and turn them into dancing halls'.[1] Kierkegaard, whose spiritual condition is difficult to ascertain, nonetheless fully realised that without preservation of a sense of sin, Christianity was doomed. Today, Kierkegaard's prophecy has become true. Having embraced hedonism, with its rehabilitation of sin and abandonment of scriptural preaching that alarms the conscience, the church has lost its function and its influence. Christ, warning of false teachers, declared: 'Do men gather grapes of thorns?' (Mt. 7:16) Proliferation of false teaching will simply make the church a futile destination for the masses. Men and women, realising that the churches profit them nothing, will abandon them.

It is not too late to restore the church to the place of integrity and power she once enjoyed. If there is to be a rescue at this eleventh hour, however, the church and the Christian must first of all take a good look at where they stand. This demands humility and honesty. Most of all, it demands courage. William Penn reflected on the state of the church in his day in his classic *No Cross, No Crown*, written while imprisoned for the faith in the Tower of London. Far from exulting in his suffering for Christ, he considered himself and his generation poor substitutes for the early Christians:

> While this integrity dwelt with Christians, mighty was the presence, and invincible the power that attended them. It quenched fire, daunted lions, turned the edge of the sword, out-faced instruments of cruelty, convicted judges, and converted

executioners. The ways their enemies sought to destroy them only increased them; and by the deep wisdom of God, those who in all their designs endeavoured to extinguish the truth were made great promoters of it.[2]

Penn traced the power of the early church to their practical holiness:

Among the faithful not a vain thought, nor an idle word, nor an unseemly action was permitted; no, not even an immodest look. There was no courtly dress, flashy apparel, flattering addresses or personal honours; much less could those lewd immoralities and scandalous vices now in vogue with Christians find either example or place among them. Their great care was not how to sport away their precious time, but how to redeem it, that they might have enough to 'work out their great salvation with fear and trembling'; not with balls and masquerades, with play-houses, dancing, feasting and gaming, no, no! To 'make their heavenly calling and election sure' was much dearer to them than the poor and trifling joys of mortality.[3]

If the presence and power that attended the early church is to be recovered, there must be an acknowledgement, as with Penn, that practical holiness and integrity is paramount. Military leaders have long known the importance of reflecting on their past mistakes. George Washington, the Commanding General of the Continental Army declared: 'To err is nature, to rectify error is glory'.[4] The writer of the Book of James, thought to be the leader of the early church in Jerusalem, compared the hearer of the Word who never changed to a person who takes a fleeting glance at their appearance in a mirror (James 1:23, 24) but goes away the same. Serious people reflect. If a Christian today in this generation would reflect on their ways, here are three key observations they might make.

The Curse of Not Knowing

Examining the assumptions that the Lord Jesus made in His warning against false teachers is a profitable exercise. Christ assumed that His hearers that day would be interested in protecting themselves and others from ravenous wolves (Mt. 7:15). He assumed an interest in whether or not Christianity and the church was in a healthy state (Mt. 7:17). He assumed that His hearers were interested in ideas or beliefs and their consequences.

For too long, Christians (and pastors especially) have abrogated their responsibility for the welfare of the whole church. Preoccupation with defending the faith against detractors, and the flock against infiltrators, has been replaced with bare sermonising. Little effort is made by leaders to discern the false ideas being daily communicated to those in their charge. The explosion of technology with its ability for messages to be spread far more easily has only exposed a failure of Christian leadership which has existed for decades: heretics and infidels having free access to the minds of unprepared congregants. The defence of many leaders is that they 'don't know' what their flock is up to – or 'didn't know' because often the damage is discovered when it's too late.

Frankly, they should know. You should know, I should know, who is talking to our flock (or our fellow Christians) and what they are saying. A Christian should know and be able to resist, insofar as they can, the false ideas of the heretical and ungodly influencers in their day. It was J. Gresham Machen who powerfully said:

> False ideas are the greatest obstacles to the reception of the gospel. We may preach with all the fervour of a reformer and yet succeed only in winning a straggler here and there, if we permit the whole collective thought of the nation or of the world to be controlled by ideas which, by the resistless force of logic, prevent Christianity from being regarded as anything more than a harmless delusion.[5]

Jesus Christ spoke so that His listeners that day on the Sermon on the Mount would be able to tell the difference between a good, or healthy, tree and a bad, or diseased, tree. He expects His followers to have a spiritual palate that discerns fruitful character and forsakes or follows accordingly.

Several years ago, a Christian couple described to me an experience they had while visiting a Christian bookshop in Northern Ireland. A large poster hung on the door advertising the latest album release from Daniel O'Donnell, available to purchase in the store. O'Donnell is a popular Irish country music singer from Co. Donegal. A Roman Catholic, he has never professed to be a Christian, is married to a divorcee, and in recent years came out in support of both same-sex marriage and abortion rights. When the couple asked the shop manager why he was selling the music of such a singer in the shop, he was antagonistic in his response. The shop owner said that he didn't know what Daniel believed and what his spiritual condition was and claimed that, if he wished to find out, he would have to meet him.

At worst, this man's answer was a blatant lie, at best a confession of gross ignorance. However, his response illustrates a hypocrisy that is widespread in Christian circles today. Pastors, preachers, elders, deacons, church administrators and lay people use a feigned ignorance of the issues and influencers of our day to exonerate themselves from responsibility. A 'don't ask, don't tell' policy is in full swing in many churches, as open sin becomes less and less difficult to disguise. Feigning ignorance, pastors shake hands with fornicators and infidels at the door of the church when the whole town is aware of their sins. They would do well to note, however, that ignorance is no excuse with God. The Scripture records such an excuse in Proverbs 24:12 ('Behold, we knew it not') and gives it no place, emphasising instead God's evaluation of our actions ('Shall not He render to every man according to his works?'). A witting or unwitting embrace of infidelity only implicates one in the sin of another (2 Jn. 1:11) and condemns both for their shared sin.

Of course, there will always be excuses to let immorality go unchecked and unrebuked. Three popular fears are widely invoked: gossip, hearsay and tittle-tattle. Gossip is described as 'informal conversation, often about other people's private affairs'. Hearsay is described as 'information you have been told but do not know to be true'. Tittle-tattle is used to describe discussion that 'is not important, and there is no real evidence that it is true'.[6] Yes, none of the above are profitable for the Christian life or compatible with Christian profession. However, neither does fear of committing any of the above relieve the Christian of his or her God-honouring duty (Job 29:16). F. W. Boreham said of Christ that 'He was never tired of pointing out that life is invariably disfigured, not so much by the wickedness that we commit by the strong hand, as by the work that we leave undone because of the weak one'.[7] Should we disobey God's clear command (Jude 3) in the name of fear, we make the same excuse as the man with one talent. Him our Lord condemned, without reserve, as 'wicked and slothful' (Mt. 25:26).

The role of the king in Hebrew society included a commitment to keep the realm safe against attack. The famous quote, 'eternal vigilance is the price of freedom' is thought to have originated from a speech made by Irishman John Philpot Curran in Dublin in 1790. Although himself a liberal and a defender of villains, there is great wisdom in Curran's words:

> It is the common fate of the indolent to see their rights become a prey to the active. The condition upon which God hath given liberty to man is eternal vigilance; which condition if he break, servitude is at once the consequence of his crime and the punishment of his guilt.[8]

Those who choose indolence as their spiritual attitude remain uninvolved while the church is shackled by imposters and false prophets. Better to follow the advice of King Solomon who declared: 'the honour of kings is to search out a matter' (Pr. 25:2).

The Curse of Not Caring

Behind a state of not knowing often lies a spirit of not caring. In the teaching profession, there is a saying which goes: 'Students don't care how much you know until they know how much you care'. To care is to be concerned. To care is to be emotionally involved in the success or failure of somebody or something. The care of the church was a daily preoccupation of Paul (2 Cor. 11:28) and the man he mentored to carry on this work, Timothy (Phil. 2:20).

Dare one assume that those Christians who do not know just might not want to know? Paul was not ignorant of the blasphemy of Hymenaeus and Alexander (1 Tim. 1:20), the apostasy of Demas (2 Tim. 4:10), or even the failure of Peter (Gal. 2:11) because he considered the welfare of the church his responsibility. Peter warned against false teachers (2 Pet. 2:1) and scoffers (2 Pet. 3:3) because he knew his life would soon be over and considered it his duty to 'stir up' the church (2 Pet. 1:13-16).

The widespread reality of spiritual lethargy in today's church speaks to a wilful carelessness on the part of many. Too many pastors are content to fill a pulpit and take a salary. Rarely, if ever, does the true spiritual condition of their congregants, let alone the wider church, cross the mind of such ministers. John the Baptist was no such fraud. On meeting the 'newly married' Herod, he did not deliver a pious platitude, assure him that God's law did not apply to him, or (as many today) congratulate him on his new adulterous relationship. Rather, he boldly declared: 'It is not lawful for thee to have thy brother's wife' (Mk. 6:18). He cared more about truth, and Herod's soul, than his next sermon. The faithful servant lost his head as a result but earned Christ's approval as the greatest of men born of women (Mt. 11:11).

To care is to challenge evil. To challenge evil is to care. Of course, Sam Allberry teaches otherwise. Living Out in one of their articles encourages Christians to adopt a lax attitude towards sexual immorality within their own homes. The blasphemous article states:

Christ's call to show hospitality and acceptance in such a situation outweighs the need to send a message about whether a sexual relationship is right or not. Church discipline is precisely that – church discipline. It can only be exercised by the church, not individuals.[9]

This shamelessly heretical comment could only originate from a mind with no fear of God or respect for His law but instead a desire to subvert the powerful testimony of Christians who do care. It articulates a philosophy that would entrap the people of God in a tomb of irrelevance.

The Scripture warns that when the soul neglects to seek out and seek after the truth, judicial blindness results. Eyes were made to see, ears to hear and minds to think, but those who neglect their use will find that God gives them over to futility (Isa. 6:10; Jn. 12:40). Their disobedience builds for them a prison of irrelevance, humiliating them before God and men. To care jealously for God's glory lies not at the periphery but at the heart of Christian service. To care jealously for God's glory will be seen primarily in a heartfelt love of all that Scripture teaches, as Christ said (Lk. 24:25-26).

During the 2016 US Presidential race, the Libertarian candidate Gary Johnson was rising in the polls until a reporter's question left him flummoxed. Asked in September 2016 about the humanitarian crisis in the war-torn Syrian city of Aleppo on MSNBC's Morning Joe, it appeared that Johnson was unaware of the city's name.[10] Misunderstanding the question, he asked, 'And what is a Lepo?' Johnson later alleged that he had merely 'blanked', but the damage was done. Subsequent polls showed Johnson's support drop to almost half of what it was before the 'Aleppo' moment.[11]

Why the plummet in support? Because knowledge of the times is a indicator of responsibility embraced. At a decisive moment in Israel's history, when it came time to transfer the kingship from King Saul to David, the men of Issachar were described as 'men that had understanding of the times, to know what Israel ought to do' (1 Chron. 12:32). They cared enough about the the welfare of the kingdom to know and model how to act at a pivotal moment.

'Blanking' is not a sign of spirituality: rather, it betrays spiritual carelessness. To be a Christian is to embrace responsibility in the world of ideas, spiritual ideas with eternal consequences. John Wesley declared, when setting the bar for his Methodist preachers: 'Ought not a Minister to have, first, a good understanding, a clear apprehension, a sound judgment, and a capacity of reasoning with some closeness?'[12] In a day when the dangers are surely even more severe than in Wesley's time, should not the bar for spiritual leadership be at least as high?

The Curse of Not Acting

Church discipline is the responsibility of all in the church. For many Christians, responding to the truth about hedonism and homosexuality may mean leaving their church or family and seeking a faithful company of believers, or acting in some other equally challenging way.

Coming out from spiritual apostasy is a difficult but imperative step if the blessing of God is to be restored to His people (2 Cor. 6:14-18). When one examines church history, the health and vitality of the church were often preserved by individual action. It was the dissenting preacher of Bedford, John Bunyan, who penned the remarkable *Pilgrim's Progress*. It was the flouting of the rules of the Church of England by John Wesley and his ordaining of Methodist preachers that reinvigorated the spiritual life of England in the 18th century. But perhaps the greatest example of a man who loved the truth enough to forsake a tyrannical church was the German Reformer Martin Luther. Philip Schaff noted that Luther regarded the summons of the Holy Roman Emperor Charles V to Worms as a 'call from God'.[13] 'His motive was not to gratify an unholy ambition', Schaff stated, 'but to bear witness to the truth'.

Luther's faith moved him beyond knowledge and concern to a conviction that he must act. What every Christian ought to know is that this conviction was not born of a preoccupation with mysticism or tradition but a thorough acquaintance with the Scriptures. Luther said no less at the Diet of Worms on Thursday, 18 April 1521, in the most memorable words he ever uttered:

> Unless I am refuted and convicted by testimonies of the Scriptures or by clear arguments… I am conquered by the Holy Scriptures quoted by me, and my conscience is bound in the word of God: I cannot and will not recant anything, since it is unsafe and dangerous to do anything against the conscience.[14]

Schaff summarised Luther's position well when he declared: 'Luther did not appeal to his conscience alone, but first and last to the Scripture as he understood it after the most earnest study'.[15] It is that earnest study of the Scriptures, and heartfelt conviction of their authority and sufficiency, which can once again disentangle the holy actors for God from the mere professors of truth.

There is a proverb in the Irish language which reads: 'Is maith an tiascaire an té atá ar an talamh'. It always brings a vivid image to my imagination, for, as a child, I illustrated this proverb for an art competition. Translated it reads, 'the best fisherman is always standing on the bridge'. The meaning of the sarcastic proverb is that those who criticise from the sidelines will always appear more able than the man in the water with the fishing rod in his hands. They will know just what he should do to catch the fish. Their self-proclaimed expertise is drowned out, however, by the fact that they have not gone to the trouble of getting wet themselves. Their feet are standing on dry ground. They have not acted. The proverb is a condemnation of human nature, with its self-deceptive ability to equate vacuous words and perpetual commentary with personal action.

Too many today are not serious in their commitment to truth. They have neglected to prioritise a systematic study of the Scriptures and a careful nurturing of their convictions. What Elijah said of the Israelites on

Mount Carmel could rightly be said of them: 'How long halt ye between two opinions? if the LORD be God, follow him: but if Baal, then follow him' (1 Kings 18:21). To halt between two opinions is to remain convinced of neither. It is the virtue of theological pacifists. It is the monstrosity of a man who will never act, because he finds the arguments for and against acting equally persuasive. He is perpetually in indecision. He is, as Nero who fiddled while Rome burned, damned as much *by* as *for* his delay. Most tragically of all, he is of no use in the hand of his Creator.

It was said of Luther that his decisiveness and conviction grew with each step he took. When Tetzel proffered his indulgences near Wittenberg in the summer of 1516, Luther felt he must do something:

> It was an irrepressible conflict of principle. He could not be silent when that barter [indulgences] was carried to the very threshold of his sphere of labour. As a preacher, a pastor, and a professor, he felt it to be his duty to protest against such measures: to be silent was to betray his theology and his conscience.[16]

Clearly, Luther's initial conviction arose from a coalescence of conditions: his pastoral responsibility, the audacity of Tetzel, and the conflict of indulgences with his own preaching combined to create an irresistible call. Luther responded in faith, but as he did, something changed: his very conviction grew. It is the scriptural paradox of those who expend strength growing stronger (Pr. 11: 24-25). Luther's certainty that the Scriptures contained authority in themselves and that the pope was not infallible increased in proportion to his obedience. Two years after Tetzel, during his debate with Cardinal Cajetan in Augsburg, Luther continued to hope for a favourable reception with the pope. However, the next year, March 1519, Luther wrote to the pope repudiating the idea of recanting.[17] Finally, while debating John Eck in Leipzig in July 1519, Luther for the first time denied both the authority of the papacy and church councils. His conviction was complete, and the road cleared to 1521, the Diet of Worms, and Europe's emancipation.

To remain, perpetually undecided, in a church from which God has long departed betrays a vacuous and divided heart. Decisiveness is born of conviction. Great military commanders have always known the value of a firm decision to inspire future courage. Such resoluteness was demonstrated in the Texas Revolution of 1836 with the burning of Vince's Bridge by General Sam Houston. The burning of the bridge before the Battle of San Jacinto made the very thought of retreat impossible, and committed Houston, psychologically as well as physically, to a victorious outcome. Soon afterwards, he routed the forces of a much larger Mexican army, heralding the end of the Texas Revolution. Houston's decisive action confirmed his unshakeable commitment to victory for a cause in which he believed.[18]

Actions speak louder than words: 'even a child is known by his doings' (Pr. 20:11). Actions speak when the time for words has passed: 'and [David] took his staff in his hand … [and] drew near to the Philistine' (1 Sam. 17:40). Actions speak when words can no longer be spoken: 'he being dead yet speaketh' (Heb. 11:4). A tragedy is befalling the church but only as long as no man or woman is willing to fight the Lord's battle and act for Him. A look at oneself, an examination of one's condition, and a determination to act in God's grace can restore the glory to God's people.

For when the moment arises, and God's people act, His enemies will be scattered. That the Lord God will preserve His church has never been in doubt. Neither is the means to that preservation. His willingness to use human instruments to accomplish His eternal purpose, God has proven again and again. As Machen asserted: 'God has always saved the Church. But He has saved it not by theological pacifists, but by sturdy contenders for the truth'.[19]

7 THINGS

TO DO

TO SAVE

YOURSELF

P AUL, WRITING IN HIS FIRST EPISTLE TO TIMOTHY, encourages him to be an example for other believers in both matters of practical conduct and in teaching. At the end of this exhortation he gives a sober command:

> Take heed unto thyself, and unto the doctrine; continue in them: for in doing this thou shalt both save thyself, and them that hear thee (1 Tim. 4:16).

Yes, the Christian is saved by faith. However, the great theologian of justification by faith, the Apostle Paul, teaches remarkably that there is a sense in which we save ourselves. Giving close attention to one's life and to faithful Christian teaching will lead one to confirm their salvation by their actions. Not only so, the hearers or followers of such a person will be equally blessed.

Here are some practical steps which may be of benefit to those blessed by this book and persuaded by its message:

1. Seek God. Knowing the true God is, in the ultimate analysis, the only thing that counts. Without an experiential knowledge of the grace of God (Rom. 3:24), all human effort is in vain.

2. Build up oneself in the faith. Study the Scripture (2 Tim. 2:15), with the aid of a systematic theology if possible. Those who are weak in their knowledge of the faith are prey to false teachers.

3. Examine your Christian life (2 Cor. 7:1). An ambivalence towards evil, whether it be the sexual sin that plagues our age, or the myriad of other sins of the flesh, is indicative of a spiritually cold heart. In particular,

the leisure pursuits of the Christian should in no sense be in places, at times, or via avenues which dishonour Christ.

4. Test the thesis of this book (1 Thess. 5:20-21). Study the teaching of the Scripture on hedonism, homosexuality, and the Christian life, and be fully convinced in your own mind of your conclusions (Rom. 14:5).

5. Speak to your pastor or minister (Gal. 6:6). Many Christians will have heard their pastor, or another church leader, speak approvingly of Piper, Allberry, or their teachings and have been alarmed. Others will have heard nothing from their pastor about this doctrinal shift and will be surprised. In both cases, discussion should be initiated with your pastor and his stance on this issue ascertained. Every Christian has a responsibility to deliver himself or herself from heresy (Rev. 18:4; Zech. 2:7) and to leave churches that have departed from the faith (Jude 3).

6. Open your mouth (Acts 17:16-17). Do not leave the 'collective thought of the nation or of the world'[1] to be dominated by the forces of evil. If you can speak, write or mount some form of protest against the evils most pressing in this age, including the promotion of homosexuality, do so.

7. Share the message of this book.

I hope this book has helped you. Should you wish to contact me, you can find me @EnochBurke or email me at info@thepiedpiperbook.com.

ACKNOWLEDGEMENTS

WRITING THIS BOOK WAS A DIFFICULT BUT BLESSED labour. However, in doing so, I entered into the labours of others (Jn. 4:38) and for their assistance I am deeply grateful.

My gracious thanks as always to my parents who raised me to 'fear God and keep His commandments' (Eccl. 12:13). My mother Martina placed the pen in my hand as a child, making the education of my siblings and I her full-time work. She has been instrumental in editing and proof-reading my work. Without her self-sacrifice, this book would not have been written – *thank you*.

I would especially like to thank Dr E. S. Williams and his wife Eileen, who provided strategic advice for much of the content of this book, as well as gracious hospitality on many occasions. My sincere thanks.

To my church who granted me time during the summer of 2019 to visit Germany and work in solitude on the first draft of this book: thank you.

Finally, to my brother Isaac for his thorough work in editing the manuscript for this book – often at short notice – my heartfelt thanks. Your work, together with the contributions of all the brothers and sisters in Christ who edited the various drafts of the manuscript, has made the final text much more readable.

May God grant it wide circulation. *Soli Deo gloria.*

ENDNOTES

Endnotes

Introduction

1   J. Gresham Machen, *Christianity and Liberalism* (Grand Rapids, MI: Eerdmans Publishing Company, 1992), 159-160.

2   See the article at German news provider Deutsche Welle, 'Germany bans gay "conversion therapy" for minors', 8 May 2020, accessed 8 July 2020, https://www.dw.com/en/germany-bans-gay-conversion-therapy-for-minors/a-53367140.

3   See the list of books distributed in 2014 here: https://t4g.org/resources/2014-book-giveaways/.

4   Philip Schaff, *History of the Christian Church Volume VII: The German Reformation* (Grand Rapids, MI: Eerdmans, 1910), 210.

5   Machen, 175.

Chapter 1: Before We Begin - Do Words Matter?

1   John Piper, *Desiring God* (Colorado Springs, CO: Multnomah, 2011), 288. This is the edition of *Desiring God* referenced throughout this book.

2   Ibid., 54

3   The definition used is found at https://www.lexico.com/definition/hedonism.

4   Nelson L. Price, *Servants not Celebrities* (Greenville, SC: Emerald House Group, 1999), 20.

5   See the analysis provided by J. P. Moreland, *Love Your God With All Your Mind* (Colorado Springs, CO: Navpress, 2012), 53.

6   Piper, 311. See also the quotation of the verse in Piper, 294.

7   Matthew Henry, *Commentary on the Whole Bible* (Peabody, MA: Hendrickson, 1994), 273.

8   James M. Rosenquist's thesis was submitted to the faculty at the Reformed Theological Seminary in Charlotte, NC in 2017. It is available (accessed July 8, 2020) at the following address, and the quotations are from pages 70 and 81: https://rts.edu/wp-content/uploads/2019/05/Rosenquist_

James_Thesis_20171025.pdf.

9   John Piper, *When I Don't Desire God* (Wheaton, IL: Crossway, 2013), 24.

10   See from 7:00 at the following video of Piper speaking at Ligonier National Conference in 2011, accessed July 8, 2020: https://www.youtube.com/watch?v=aOEonzhUNaA.

11   Ibid.

12   Quoted in W. Carlos Martyn, *The Life and Times of Martin Luther* (New York: American Tract Society), 474.

13   See the title of Chapter 5 in Piper's book: 'Scripture: Kindling for Christian Hedonism'.

14   Piper, 17.

15   Ibid., 18.

16   *The Shorter Catechism* (Carlisle, PA: Banner of Truth), 1.

17   Martin Luther, 'To the Councilmen of All Cities in Germany That They Establish and Maintain Christian Schools', 366.

18   William Hendriksen, *New Testament Commentary: 1 & 2 Timothy and Titus* (London: Banner of Truth, 1972), 367.

19   Piper, 308.

20   C.S. Lewis, *Letters to Malcolm: Chiefly on Prayer* (New York: Harcourt Brrace Jovanovich, 1963), 90, quoted in Piper, 309.

21   C.S. Lewis, *Mere Christianity* (London: Fontana Books, 1961), 91.

22   Ibid., 99.

23   Piper, 309-310.

24   Vernard Eller, *The Simple Life* (Grand Rapids, MI: Eerdmans, 1973), 121-122.

25   See the collection of Eller's works online. This reference can be accessed at http://www.hccentral.com/eller1/cc122767.html.

26   See the chapter 'Anarchic Theology and Arky Politics' in Vernard Eller, *Christian Theology: Jesus' Primacy over the Powers* (Grand Rapids, MI: Eerdmans, 1987), available at http://www.hccentral.com/eller12/part7.html.

27 See Piper's comments at a Q&A session in Los Angeles, CA in February 2010, available at https://www.youtube.com/watch?v=X3tWD1MZrQ8.

28 See Rose French, 'Key Minnesota Pastors Opt Out of Marriage Fight', 2 September 2012, http://www.startribune.com/key-minnesota-pastors-opt-out-of-marriage-fight/159819565/. John Piper stated in a sermon before the vote 'Don't press the organization of the church or her pastors into political activism'. See Jonathan Parnell, 'Your Pastor Is Not Your Political Activist', 24 June 2012, https://www.desiringgod.org/articles/your-pastor-is-not-your-political-activist.

Chapter 2: John Piper - Preaching Mysticism, Not Christ

1 Piper, *Desiring God*, 28.

2 Ibid., 18.

3 Ibid., 23.

4 Ibid., 24.

5 Ibid., 18.

6 See the transcript of Piper's address at Passion 2020 which is available at https://www.desiringgod.org/messages/live-for-your-greatest-desire.

7 These words appear on the blurb for Piper's book *Desiring God* (Colorado Springs, CO: Multnomah, 2011).

8 Earle E. Cairns, *Church History Through the Centuries* (Grand Rapids, MI: Zondervan, 1996), 242.

9 See the book chapter from Thanissaro Bhikkhu entitled 'Desire and Imagination in the Buddhist Path', accessed July 4, 2020, available at https://www.dhammatalks.org/books/PurityOfHeart/Section0007.html.

10 Piper, 90-92.

11 Arthur L. Johnson, *Faith Misguided: Exposing the Dangers of Mysticism* (Chicago: Moody Press, 1988), 133.

12 Ibid., 39.

13 Ibid., 144.

14 Loraine Boettner, *Roman Catholicism* (Phillipsburg, NJ: Presbyterian and Reformed Publishing Company, 1962), 89.

15 Schaff, 22.

16 Ibid., 25.

17 Ibid., 142.

18 Ibid., 31.

19 Johnson, 143.

20 Ibid., 38.

21 John Calvin, *Institutes of the Christian Religion* (Peabody, MA: Hendrickson Publishers, 2008), 43.

22 Ibid., 765.

23 Vatican Ecumenical Council I Decrees, Session 4: 18 July 1870 - First Dogmatic Constitution on the Church of Christ, Chap. I, http://www.intratext.com/IXT/ENG0063/_PH.HTM, accessed July 4, 2020.

24 Vatican Ecumenical Council I Decrees, Session 4: 18 July 1870 - First Dogmatic Constitution on the Church of Christ, http://www.intratext.com/IXT/ENG0063/_PD.HTM, accessed July 4, 2020.

25 Schaff, 257.

26 Ibid., 228.

27 Ibid., 248.

28 Ibid., 252.

29 Calvin, 735.

30 Ibid.

31 Ibid., 757.

32 John Piper, 'If You Had Two Minutes to Talk With the Pope, What Would You Say to Him?', 15 December 2009, accessed July 4, 2020, https://www.desiringgod.org/interviews/if-you-had-two-minutes-to-talk-with-the-pope-what-would-you-say-to-him.

33 Calvin, 801.

34 Ibid., 739.

35 Ibid., 691.

36   Ibid., 758.

37   John Piper, 'Contrary to Roman Catholics, the Bible is Our Sufficient Authority', 28 October 2016, accessed July 4, 2020, https://www.desiringgod.org/interviews/contrary-to-roman-catholics-the-bible-is-our-sufficient-authority.

38   John H. Gerstner, *A Primer on Roman Catholicism* (Morgan, PA: Soli Deo Gloria Publications, 1995), 31.

39   Ibid., 33.

40   Ibid.

41   John Piper, 'Can a Devout Roman Catholic Be Genuinely Born Again?', 21 February 2018, accessed July 4, 2020, https://www.desiringgod.org/interviews/can-a-devout-roman-catholic-be-genuinely-born-again.

42   Schaff, 181.

43   Ibid., 7.

44   Gerstner, 40.

Chapter 3: Preaching Christ, Not Mysticism

1   Ibid.

2   By the term 'Romanism' in this book is meant what Schaff described as 'the Latin church turned against the Reformation, consolidated by the Council of Trent and completed by the Vatican Council of 1870 with its dogman of papal absolutism and papal infallibility'. See Schaff, 4.

3   Boettner, 456.

4   Linleigh J. Roberts, *Let Us Make Man* (Carlisle, PA: Banner of Truth, 1988), 106-107.

5   Ibid., 107.

6   Piper devotes a whole chapter in *Desiring God* to conversion, entitled 'Conversion: The Creation of a Christian Hedonist', 53.

7   Ibid., 71.

8   Ibid., 71-72.

9   Roberts, 108.

10   Piper, 299.

11   Ibid.

12   Ibid., 300.

13   Arthur W. Pink, *The Life of Faith* (Ross-shire, Scotland: Christian Focus Publications, 2011), 92.

14   Piper, 301.

15   Andrew R. Fausset, *Commentary on Judges* (Carlisle, PA: Banner of Truth, 1999), 256.

16   Ibid., 258.

17   Ibid.

18   Ibid., 315.

19   Schaff, 17.

Chapter 4: Allberry - Turning Grace Into Lasciviousness

1   F. LaGard Smith, *Sodom's Second Coming* (Eugene, OR: Harvest House Publishers, 1993), 245.

2   This speech is available at the Vimeo account of Bethlehem College & Seminary, accessed July 4, 2020, https://vimeo.com/54488097.

3   See the article on the Desiring God website, 'Homophobia Has No Place in the Church', March 29, 2016, accessed July 4, 2020, https://www.desiringgod.org/articles/homophobia-has-no-place-in-the-church.

4   See the definition of *reprobate* in Nelson's *New Illustrated Bible Dictionary* (Nashville, TN: Thomas Nelson, 2014).

5   These are available on the Living Out website 'What we're about' page, accessed July 4, 2020, https://www.livingout.org/what-we-re-about.

6   The definition used is from the Collins Dictionary Online, accessed July 8, 2020, available at https://www.collinsdictionary.com/dictionary/english/paradigm-shift.

7   The speech by Sam Allberry is available here, accessed July 8, 2020, https://www.youtube.com/watch?v=O7K608T7MdA&feature=youtu.be

8   The references to Allberry's book are the Kindle edition. This reference is Sam Allberry, *Is God Anti-Gay?* (Epsom, UK: The Good Book Company, 2013), 7/82, i.e. page 7 out of 82.

9   Allberry, 59/82.

10   Ibid., 7/82.

11   Ibid., 51/82.

12   Dave Breese, *Seven Men Who Rule the World From the Grave* (Chicago: Moody Press, 1990), 204.

13   Allberry, 34/82.

14   Ibid., 54/82'

15   Ibid., 52/82.

16   Ibid., 55/82.

17   D. Martyn Lloyd-Jones, *Spiritual Depression: Its Causes and Cures* (London: Marshall Pickering, 1998), 28.

18   Allberry, 18/82.

19   Ibid., 16/82.

20   Ibid., 9/82.

21   Ibid., 56/82.

22   Ibid., 27/82.

23   Ibid., 10/82.

24   These comments were made by Allberry during a Questions and Answers Session filmed by the ERLC in 2015. The ERLC is the public policy arm of the Southern Baptist Convention. The video is available at the following link on Youtube, accessed July 8, 2020, https://www.youtube.com/watch?v=RL40YoUYh6o&feature=youtu.be

25   The article in referred to is available at the following link, accessed July 8, 2020, https://www.livingout.org/resources/becoming-christians-what-if-you-are-an-ssa-couple. The interview where Allberry made the comment was The Gospel Coalition 2019 National Conference in Indianapolis, Indiana and is available at the following link, accessed July 8, 2020, https://vimeo.com/327878051

26   Accessed July 8, 2020, 'The Heterosexual Gospel', September 4, 2018, https://www.desiringgod.org/articles/the-heterosexual-gospel

Chapter 5: Rescuing Grace from Lasciviousness

1   Accessed July 8, 2020, 'What does the Bible say about homosexuality?', https://www.livingout.org/the-bible-and-ssa.

2   This comment is at approximately 7:45 during the 2014 session with Al Mohler, Sam Allberry, and Russell Moore. The video is available on YouTube, accessed July 8, 2020, https://www.youtube.com/watch?v=s7Ri3phs1nc.

3   See 29:50 at the same link, https://www.youtube.com/watch?v=s7Ri3phs1nc.

4   See the 'If your child is an adult' subsection of the following article on the Living Out website, accessed July 8, 2020, https://www.livingout.org/resources/how-should-i-respond-if-my-child-comes-out-to-me. Note that I refer to this article again in the final chapter of this book.

5   See the Question and Answer available at https://www.shortercatechism.com/resources/wsc/wsc_083.html.

6   Jonathan Edwards, *A History of the Work of Redemption Containing the Outlines of a Body of Divinity* (Philadelphia: Presbyterian Board of Publication), 64.

7   Allberry, *Is God Anti-Gay?* (2013, Kindle Edition), 27/82.

8   See the speech given by Katherine Zappone on May 17, 2015, accessed July 8, 2020, https://christchurchcathedral.ie/worship/sermons/promise-freedom-address-idahot-day-senator-katherine-zappone/. Christ Church Cathedral, on whose website the speech is posted, is an Anglican cathedral in Dublin, Ireland.

9   The website is still available online at the time of printing, accessed July 8, 2020, https://www.katherinezappone2020.ie/

10   The quotes from Allberry in this section, unless otherwise referenced, are taken from his article on the Living Out website, 'What does the Bible say about homosexuality?', accessed July 23, 2020, https://www.livingout.org/the-bible-and-ssa.

11   Allberry, *Is God Anti-Gay?*, 8/82.

12   Ibid., 51/82.

13   James Barmby, *The Pulpit Commentary: Romans* (London: Funk & Wagnalls, 1906), 11.

14   Allberry, 25/82.

15   Charles Hodge, *A Commentary on Romans* (Carlisle, PA: Banner of Truth, 1975), 39.

16   Robert Haldane, *The Epistle to the Romans* (London: Banner of Truth, 1966), 64.

17   Louis Berkhof, *A Summary of Christian Doctrine* (Carlisle, PA: Banner of Truth, 1960), 68.

18   Allberry, 44/82.

19   Boettner, 183.

20   Ibid.

21   See Article 2359 which states 'Homosexual persons are called to chastity', accessed July 8, 2020, https://www.vatican.va/archive/ccc_css/archive/catechism/p3s2c2a6.htm.

22   I first came across this analogy in the chapter 'The Nature of New Testament Eschatology' in Anthony Hoekema, *The Bible and the Future* (Grand Rapids, MI: Eerdmans Publishing Company, 1994), 21. Hoekema attributes this analogy to theologian Oscar Cullmann.

23   Hoekema, *The Christian Looks At Himself* (Grand Rapids, MI: Eerdmans Publishing Company, 1975), 44-45.

24   Ibid., 45-46.

25   Ibid., 46-47.

26   Ibid.

27   Ibid., 58]

28   The author of 'O Little Town of Bethlehem' and the primer *Lectures on Preaching*, the 19th century clergyman Phillips Brooks, famously declared 'Truth through Personality is our description of real preaching' in *Lectures on Preaching* (London: Griffith *et al*, 1886), 8.

29   Susannah Wesley, quoted in Michael Reagan and Bob Phillips, *The*

All-American Quote Book (Eugene, OR: Harvest House Publishers, 1995), 135.

30   Lloyd-Jones, *Spiritual Depression*, 60.

31   Ibid.

32   Ibid., 62.

Chapter 6: Holiness Not Hedonism

1   The performance of Hillsong at Passion 2020 is online, accessed July 8, 2020, https://www.youtube.com/watch?v=Hb9xYyYNn7k&t=231s.

2   See Christine Caine's speech at Passion 2020, available online, accessed July 8, 2020, https://www.youtube.com/watch?v=0Ai2ukyggLo

3   David A. Noebel, *The Battle for Truth* (Eugene, OR: Harvest House Publishers, 2001), 99.

4   See Yaron Steinbuch, 'Black Lives Matter co-founder describes herself as "trained Marxist"', New York Post, June 25, 2020, accessed July 8, 2020, https://nypost.com/2020/06/25/blm-co-founder-describes-herself-as-trained-marxist/

5   Bill Flax, 'Do Marxism and Christianity Have Anything in Common?', Forbes.com, May 12, 2011, accessed July 8, 2020, https://www.forbes.com/sites/billflax/2011/05/12/do-marxism-and-christianity-have-anything-in-common/#7cb114976877.

6   C. Allyn Russell, *Voices of American Fundamentalism* (Philadelphia: The Westminster Press, 1976), 203.

7   Ibid.

8   Ibid., 203-204.

9   Ibid., 198.

10   Machen, *Christianity and Liberalism*, 177.

11   A video of the interview can be found on YouTube, accessed July 8, 2020, https://www.youtube.com/watch?v=4Yhn_4mmowU.

12   This message appears to be no longer on the Desiring God website. However, it can be viewed at the following link, with the Desiring God logo displayed clearly at the beginning of the video, accessed July 8, 2020, https://

www.youtube.com/watch?v=A20Og3LoIko.

13   See the product description for the book *Dug Down Deep* (Multnomah, 2011) on Amazon, which includes the following review from John Piper: 'I love the term "humble orthodoxy." And I love Josh Harris. When they come together (Josh and humble orthodoxy), as they do in this book, you get a humble, helpful, courageous testimony to biblical truth. Thank you, Josh, for following through so well on the conversation in Al Mohler's study', accessed July 8, 2020, https://www.amazon.co.uk/Dug-Down-Deep-Joshua-Harris/dp/1601423713.

14   See the account provided at Christianity Today, 'Polycarp: Aged Bishop of Smyrna', accessed July 8, 2020, https://www.christianitytoday.com/history/people/martyrs/polycarp.html.

15   See the definition provided on BibleHub.com, accessed July 8, 2020, https://biblehub.com/greek/53.htm.

16   C. H. Spurgeon, *The Sword and the Trowel*, August 1887, footnote in *C.H. Spurgeon Autobiography: Vol. 1 – The Early Years* (Carlisle, PA: Banner of Truth, 2011), 471.

17   C.H. Spurgeon, 'Another Word Concerning the Downgrade', from the August 1887 edition of *The Sword and the Trowel*, accessed July 8, 2020, https://archive.spurgeon.org/s_and_t/dg03.php.

18   Josiah G. Holland, 'God, give us men!', accessed July 8, 2020, https://www.theotherpages.org/poems/holland1.html.

Chapter 7: Taking a Look at Ourselves

1   Søren Kierkegaard, *Søren Kierkegaard Skrifter* vol. 25, (Copenhagen: Gads Forlag, 1997-2013), 20, 69, 79.

2   William Penn, *No Cross No Crown* (Akron, Ohio: Market Street Fellowship, 2017), 29.

3   Ibid., 30.

4   This comment is reputed to have been made by Washington to William Payne in 1754.

5   This quote is from an address delivered on September 20, 1912, at the opening of the 101st session of Princeton Theological Seminary. The address is reprinted in J. Gresham Machen, *What is Christianity?* (Grand Rapids, MI: Eerdmans Publishing Company, 1951), 156-169; the quote is on page 162.

6   Definitions from Collins Online Dictionary.

7   F. W. Boreham, *The Tide Comes In*, 61-62, as quoted in *Daily Readings from F. W. Boreham* (London: Hodder and Stoughton, 1976), 114.

8   J. P. Curran, 'Election of Lord Mayor of Dublin', speech before the Privy Council, July 10, 1790. From Thomas Davis (ed) (1847) *The Speeches of the Right Honorable John Philpot Curran*, 103-131 (archive.org). Quote is from p. 105.

9   See the 'If your child is an adult' subsection of the following article on the Living Out website, accessed July 8, 2020, https://www.livingout.org/resources/how-should-i-respond-if-my-child-comes-out-to-me.

10   The incident is available on the MSNBC YouTube channel, accessed July 9, 2020, https://www.youtube.com/watch?v=fOT_BoGpCn4.

11   See The Washington Post, Oct 24, 2016, 'Gary Johnson's poll collapse is happening as predicted', accessed July 8, 2020, https://www.washingtonpost.com/news/the-fix/wp/2016/10/24/gary-johnsons-poll-collapse-is-happening-as-predicted/.

12   John Wesley, 'An Address to the Clergy,' in *The Works of John Wesley* 3d ed. (Grand Rapids, MI: Baker, 1979), 481.

13   Schaff, 294.

14   Ibid., 304.

15   Ibid., 313.

16   Ibid., 154.

17   Ibid., 177.

18   Nelson Price recounts this story in Price, *Servants, Not Celebrities*, 19.

19   Machen, *Chrisitanity and Liberalism*, 174.

Conclusion

1   Machen, *What is Christianity?*, 162.

INDEX

Printed in Great Britain
by Amazon

26633513R00096